RESCUE US WISDOM

GIANTS DO FALL

(Primer Version)

TIMOTHY D. RICHARD

ISBN 979-8-88685-262-2 (paperback)
ISBN 979-8-88685-263-9 (digital)

Christian Faith Publishing
832 Park Avenue
Meadville, PA 16335
www.christianfaithpublishing.com

Printed in the United States of America

CONTENTS

INTRODUCTION

America is more divided than ever before. Negativity abounds. Violence is everywhere. The inner workings of our government seem under attack.

Will it ever get better? What's truth anymore? There are heated fingers pointing in the political realm. People everywhere bicker.

Issues divide us. What is right? What is wrong? What direction is our nation headed?

Is God really in control? Is there a God? If there was, is he dead?

What is the purpose of life? Why do we die? What happens when we die?

It seems we have more questions than answers. A main one right now is will life ever get back to normal. What is normal?

Is our country headed for peril? Is our "democracy" in jeopardy?

King Solomon was extremely wise. Though he lived long ago his wisdom speaks into present times. The questions of our age receive answers. Many readers of this book will agree.

Rescue Us Wisdom: Giants Do Fall (Primer Version) is a compact summary of the original book sprinkled with additional truth.

Youth to our oldest seniors can benefit from this writing. That is my hope and aim.

The thirsty find living water. The hungry are filled with the bread of life. The ones desiring heavenly gifts can ask for them.

Be richly blessed.

1

KING SOLOMON'S COURT

A long time ago, in ancient times, there was a famous court case recorded in scripture.

Two moms both claimed to be an infant's mother. The child was only three days old when he was abducted. The two women were living in the same house. One mom's child accidentally died. Then she snuck into the other woman's room at night and swapped her dead baby for the other mom's living one.

In the morning the real mom discovered her baby was dead. But then in better light it was clear what really happened. The dead child was not hers. She knew it was the other woman's baby. The switch happened in the dark when she was sleeping.

She confronted the other woman, but the woman lied. She denied she switched babies.

The real mom was scared. The other woman would not give her baby back, and not only that, was telling everyone the real mom was the liar.

Later, and scripture doesn't say how long it took, the case goes before King Solomon. He is the wise son of the previous king, King David, who is a well-known bible figure.

2

KING DAVID'S VICTORY

King David was the one who, as a young man, fought a one-on-one battle with a ten-foot-tall giant of a man. Goliath was a mighty, seasoned warrior, decked out with the most modern armor of the time.

David, on the other hand, was a shepherd boy. He tended a few sheep out in a field near his home. You have to understand this was about three thousand years ago, and civilization of the time did not have electricity or mechanized transportation.

There were no cars, no phones, no indoor plumbing, no factories making furniture, televisions, modern beds, clocks, and no internet, computers, or much of anything.

Cups and plates were made by hand from clay on a potter's wheel. Wine was kept in specially prepared animal skins. Wheat was ground into powder by hand and baked in a wood fired oven.

Soldiers battled with bows and arrows, spears, knives, and swords. There were no guns or modern weapons.

Now get this. David went into battle with a sling and stones. His enormous opponent was protected head to toe in a steel suit of armor.

What makes the story even more amazing is, if David lost, his whole army must surrender to the other army. That means they would be hauled off to the other army's country and become lifetime slaves.

The king asked among his ranks for a volunteer to fight Goliath. There were no takers. Every day that monstrously tall foe stood up with a puffed chest and trash-talked. He called the Army of the Israelites cowards and insulted them. The stakes were high. Challenge and lose to him, and all of your comrades lose their freedom.

David wasn't a soldier. But he had older brothers there on the front line. He was sent to them by his dad. David was dispatched to bring them food and find out if they were okay. There were no phones. He walked a long distance to find out how they were doing.

David arrived. He gave his food to the supply master, the one in charge of the food. Then he went to look for his brothers. Nearing them, Goliath showed up to shout his daily obscenities at the Israeli army. David was angered. He took offense, so much so, he became infuriated. He spouted off to the soldiers near his brothers.

The King of the Israelites promised all kinds of rewards for anyone who took on this brute and whipped him.

The King received notice of David's righteous distain for the giant. He sent for him, and the two talked. He could see David was still a boy, but David had spunk and courage. David had grit. David told him, I've killed lions and bears. This guy doesn't scare me. God has delivered me from fierce animals. He'll give me victory over this beast too.

Likely a shock to the entire army, David was selected to fight Goliath to the death. Imagine David's brothers and the other Israeli troops' reactions. Here's a shepherd boy, without armor, moving to the battleground area to confront the opposing army's mightiest warrior.

He loses, and we're all going to be enslaved. We lose our freedom. What will become of our families left behind? Who will provide for and protect them? What is the king thinking by sending this boy against that tower of a man?

Goliath entered the battleground protected by his steel armor. David was dressed in his shepherd's garb. It's how he normally dressed. He tried on the king's armor at the suggestion of the king. The items were too heavy and clunky to wear. He took them off.

David decided to fight as he knows how. He took with him his sling and selected five smooth stones from a nearby stream.

Goliath's spear shank was likely about as round as most men's arms. It's got a razor-sharp steel point on the end of a long thick shaft. And the guy intended to ram it straight through David's unprotected body.

Goliath was eager. He saw this kid come out against him and he's spewing vulgar insults. He's outraged. A boy? He yelled how he's going to mutilate David.

David was not deterred. He fired back his declaration of victory. He verbally assaulted Goliath. He shouted God has delivered me from other beasts. He will deliver me from you. Then everyone will know there is a God in Israel.

Goliath charged. David advances too. He whirled his sling loaded with the first smooth stone. While swiftly coming at Goliath, he let the stone go. The release hurled it with incredible force and accuracy. It struck the behemoth just under the helmet rim in the brow. It's lights out. Goliath face plants mid-stride. He never saw it coming.

David continued his quick advance and reached the brute. He picked up Goliath's own sword, huge compared to a normal one, and brought it down hard. If Goliath wasn't deceased from the stone's impact, he was now. The mouth that flapped insults moments earlier was separated from the body at the neck. Giants do fall.

What a rousing victory. David and the army glorified the Lord in Heaven for the success. The opposing army, stunned by their hero's death, made a run for it.

Apparently, they had no intention of surrendering if Goliath died. By running, they broke their promise. They couldn't run fast enough to escape. They were wiped out. It was total victory.

3

BRILLIANT WISDOM

Now back to the story about the two moms. King Solomon, who acquired the throne after his dad David died from old age, was very wise. He's the wisest man ever known to live before Jesus.

Scripture doesn't say so, but it likely took a long time for the two moms to come before him to decide the case. We can think of his court as we view the United States Supreme Court. Only the most important cases that the lower courts can't get right come before him.

This suggests the real mom has been separated from her child for quite some time. How agonizing this must be. She hurt deeply. She missed holding him, nursing him, kissing him, smiling at him, and receiving his affection back.

All the while the impostor mom had been lying. She said it was her child. She said the other mom was a liar. She probably makes up other lies too.

Lies are not from God. Scripture says so. People shouldn't lie. After being caught in lies, a person cannot be trusted to ever be telling the truth.

The king listened to both women say—I'm the real mom. It's the other woman who is the liar.

Guess what? One of them is being truthful. The other one is a liar. But which one is which?

The wise king gets a brilliant thought. It became his secret plan. He commanded a court guard to cut the child in two and give each woman half. He announced his decision loud and clear to the two women. Neither of them knew it was just a test.

The real mom panicked. No, king, she pleaded. Do not kill the child, let him live. I beg you, give the child to the other woman.

The impostor mom had a completely different reply. Unbelievably, she agreed with the king. Yes, king, cut the child in two so neither she nor I will have him.

> *(1 Kings 3:26) The woman whose son was alive was deeply moved out of love for her son and said to the king, "Please, my lord, give her the living baby! Don't kill him!" But the other said, "Neither I nor you shall have him. Cut him in two!"*

What a bizarre reaction. The impostor mom wanted to kill a child to settle an argument.

Well, the strategy of the king worked. The real mom was the one willing to give up her child to preserve his life. That's true love. The other woman, the impostor mom—well, that's what you call hate. Those promoting death to a child are not on the side of God.

4

WISDOM SPEAKS TRUTH

The reason for telling the impostor mom story is to bring wisdom from three thousand years ago into current times. Our nation is very divided. We are divided by political party. We are divided by skin color and religion. We are divided by problems in society and what to do about it. Who is right? Who is wrong?

Actually, King Solomon's wisdom makes it very easy to know. The same impostor mom voice is heard in society today. She stands in American courts and insists—cut the child in two. These are the most innocent babies imaginable. They are still in their mother's wombs.

When a woman of any age gets pregnant, the baby starts as an embryo. Cells divide at rapid speed. Special medical instruments used in a certain way detect a heartbeat in only three weeks. Body parts are already forming, although super tiny.

The impostor mom in the King Solomon court case was a liar. To protect her lie, her main strategy was to say the real mom is the liar.

The wisdom of King Solomon exposed her. Now the same wisdom exposes the liar impostor in abortion. Amazing.

5

TRUTH VS. LIES

The majority of Americans—nearly nine of every ten of us—believe in God. Some have strong belief, some not so strong, some weak belief, and finally, a small amount no belief.

God is the creator of life. The devil loves death. Lucifer the devil won death in the Garden of Eden when he tricked Adam and Eve to eat the forbidden fruit. Up until then, there was no death. They were going to live forever.

Jesus came to earth long after the days of Adam and Eve. He came to show the love of His Father in Heaven. The Father sent his Son to conquer death. Jesus healed people and taught about God's love. He informed his closest followers the truths about good and evil.

It all got put into the bible for us to learn. Understand truth from words spoken by Jesus about the devil.

(John 8:44)… When he lies, he speaks his native language, for he is a liar and the father of lies.

The devil teaches how to lie. He makes people believe abortion is a loving way to end a pregnancy. The devil gets a small number of Americans to insist there is no God, or if there was a God, he is dead.

The impostor devil lies to humanity. One lie says it's okay to end a child's life in the womb.

Jesus spoke about contrasting himself to evil. Let's see what it says.

(John 10:10) The thief comes only to steal and kill and destroy; I have come that they may have life, and have it to the full.

The impostor is much more than a liar. He's a thief. He comes to steal the living baby from moms' wombs by telling her all kinds of lies, like it isn't a baby until it's born or you're too young to have a baby. You can have another baby when you're older.

Or you're too poor to raise a baby, or you have enough children, or you should finish college first. A child right now is too soon; it will ruin your life. All kinds of lies get moms to think it must be okay to abort.

Even after rape or incest-rape the child has a purpose to fulfill on earth. Giving away the baby to another mom blesses her and the child.

Moms aborting after rape and incest-rape experience the same emotional hurts as all women. She weeps she did not protect her child, regardless of how it was conceived.

Lies say family incest pregnancies cause severe birth defects. Science simply does not support the claim.

Years ago, technology was not advanced. Liars lied by saying the developing child was a blob of tissue. That is untrue. Science of today proves it.

Liars continue to speak other lies. One of them is it's your body, you get to choose. For followers of Jesus, that is untrue. Scripture is very clear.

> *(1 Corinthians 6:19–20) Do you not know that your bodies are temples of the Holy Spirit, who is in you, whom you have received from God? You are not your own; you were bought at a price. Therefore honor God with your bodies.*

Scripture is very clear for followers of Jesus. Our bodies are no longer our own. He died on the cross in our place to purchase our redemption. Bodies become a temple for the Holy Spirit.

The impostor liars insist women get to make the choice. Well, just because the impostors created a law and impostor judges enforce them, doesn't mean God agrees.

This goes for sex too. God says it belongs in marriage. The impostor spirit says have fun, you're only young once. That's the same spirit's voice that says your body is your own and have an abortion if you get pregnant.

None of it is from God.

Modern day prophets are saying abortion must stop. We are supposed to be a godly nation. We are to turn back to God and unify.

Find prophetic voices at Elijah Streams, Elijah Fire, Sid Roth, and the Victory Chanel—Flashpoint.

God has such deep love and grace for someone who is sorry for having an abortion. That extends to those who led somebody to have one, performed one, or taught they are okay. Now is the time for the lies to end. Anyone that goes on purposely lying will not be viewed kindly from Heaven.

6

IMPOSTOR SPIRIT

The impostor spirit intends to control certain states of America and keep abortion going there, even if the United States Supreme Court strikes down abortion at the national level.

Not only that, impostors push online abortion pills to take at home. This causes the baby to slowly die in the womb. Many moms bleed dangerously afterward, and some have died or almost died. It's really quite tragic.

Many people are fooled by impostors.

Others know better and participate willingly. This does not please God.

Hearts and people change. Wisdom brings hidden things to light. Then the new choice is to accept or reject wisdom.

The impostor spirit desires the world contain no more than five hundred million people. Our current earthly population is 7.5 billion. Doing the math, impostor spirit elitists want only a fraction of us to remain. More than ninety percent of earth's population, they desire to die.

If we die from disease, from an abortion, get shot in a gang war, perish from drug overdose, or die in any other way, it is one less of us on earth.

Many deaths come from starvation in foreign lands. The same nations have many get sick from impure water. Impostors don't care. Aid sent from the US or other countries gets stolen. Remember, impostors steal, kill, and destroy. Some aid gets through. Much does not.

Impostor elitists desire to replace the ten commandments given to Moses by God. The Georgia Guidestones are the ten commandments of the New World Order.

One of them desires earth's population be maintained to 500 million people.

Proverbs, chapter eight, wraps up with contrast between good and evil.

> *(Proverbs 8:34–36) Blessed are those who listen to me, watching daily at my doors, waiting at my doorway. For those who find me find life and receive favor from the Lord. But those who fail to find me harm themselves; all who hate me love death.*

Verse 35 says those who find wisdom, find life. Verse 36 says those who hate wisdom love death.

God's love and the impostor spirit are summed up right there.

Jesus and wisdom are synonymous terms. Those who love Jesus, love life.

The impostor spirit loves death because it hates Jesus.

The New World Order pretends love. However, they love abortion. They are aligned to the impostor spirit. They desire over ninety percent of us to perish.

Greater than thirty percent of the earth's inhabitants say they follow Jesus. That's two and a half billion people. Impostors want Christians dead. After that they desire almost five billion more people to die.

Impostor elitists promote abortion to minimize world population. They privately snicker at how easy it is to trick people.

Lies keep their message of hate appearing like a message of hope for girls and women who find themselves in desperation.

Females can become pregnant unexpectedly. They panic. It wasn't supposed to happen. They don't know what to do. It's embarrassing to admit being pregnant. It seems better to keep it hidden.

They receive bad advice. Have an abortion and your life goes back to normal.

It doesn't. Girls and women realize it was a baby after all. Many are crushed. They wish they hadn't done it.

Many begin a lifetime of regret. The thought of what happened haunts them. It's a painful memory. They keep silent. Many fear judgments if they speak about it.

Abortion can affect women and men in ways they do not understand. The official term is post-traumatic stress disorder (PTSD).

7

GOOD NEWS ABOUT THE UNBORN

There is good news. God is a compassionate God. Any mom can be reunited in Heaven with her unborn child. God adopts all unborn children. This is true for miscarries, stillborn, and the aborted. The innocent babies reside in Heaven.

> *(Psalm 37:18) The blameless spend their days under the Lord's care, and their inheritance will endure forever.*

All living people can become blameless too. Anyone who asks Jesus to forgive their sins and come into their heart is saved by him.

Deep emotional hurts can be purged from one's soul. Praying Medic produced a compact biblical booklet of easy steps to follow. It is important to ask for joy to replace sorrow. Asking is how it is given. He points out the process described in the booklet does not replace the work of licensed health care providers.

Revelator Kat Kerr says we can remove wounds from our soul. This includes abortion trauma. We use the keys of the kingdom as found in Matthew.

> *(Matthew 16:19) I will give you the keys of the kingdom of heaven; whatever you bind on earth will be bound in heaven, and whatever you loose on earth will be loosed in heaven.*

We choose by our will to loose the emotional hurts from abortion, death of loved ones, physical or verbal abuse, horror and violence watched in TV shows or movies, addictions, porn, witchcraft, tarot card readings, psychic readings, Ouija boards, and anything satanic.

People having nightmares for years, and addictions, have been delivered from them instantly doing Heaven's soul-cleansing according to Kat. Find her on the internet.

Here is an example:

> *Father God, I choose from my will to loose all harmful things from my soul, of what I've experienced or seen, wounds from lies or deception, bad things spoken over me, or any other darkness that entered me in ways I do not understand, in Jesus's name. Amen.*

When she leads groups to repeat after her, she names all the things individually, like abortion, addictions, death of loved ones, TV or movie violence, witchcraft, etc.

She says to wait a couple of minutes for Heaven to purge darkness. Then it is necessary to fill the void. Kat says binding God to our soul is very powerful. Below is an example.

> *Father, bind to my soul the love of God, the life of God, the plans of God, His joy, His peace, and His divine health. In Jesus's name. Amen.*

This binds to our soul the wonderful things of God to prosper our life.

8

SCIENCE IS ALWAYS ON GOD'S SIDE

Impostors promote falsehood through lies.

Science is always on God's side. Impostors know this. They twist science to promote their false messages.

Abortion is an easy example. For years the impostor spirit claimed the child was a blob of cells. Science proves the cells are forming into arms and legs and a heartbeat already in three weeks.

Science exposes impostor's lies. Then impostors change their justification. They change course. First the unborn baby was a blob of cells. Now impostors say the female gets to decide what is best for her body. As already refuted, scripture says the opposite.

Our body is not our own. Jesus paid for us on the cross. We are to honor God with our bodies.

God created us. Why would he want a child extracted from the womb so it couldn't be born? It's illogical. But impostors speak illogically and con people to believe it.

Climate change is another example. Impostors hide the true data. Scientists have collected climate data for about one hundred fifty years. Impostors will hide most of the data and select a portion of it to make their case.

Scientists know from fossil records and carbon dating many dinosaurs lived and died in the South Dakota Badlands when it was a lush, tropical, water filled area.

Tropical? Like Central America? Way up north near the chilly Canadian border? Our earth can heat up many degrees and still not approach what it was millions of years ago when dinosaurs lived. Impostors claim a half decree change will be catastrophic.

There are two choices. Trust God, or trust impostors. Impostors, who claim abortion is compassion, also claim the world will end soon if climate isn't urgently addressed. Nonsense.

What is the impostor motive in this cause? To divert trillions of US dollars out of the US to fund their diabolical schemes. They steal our tax money to destroy us.

(Proverbs 29:16) When the wicked thrive, so does sin, but the righteous will see their downfall.

Jesus said we can tell who is from God and who is not, from a tree's fruit. A good tree does not have bad fruit, and a bad tree does not have good fruit.

Abortion is bad fruit. All fruit on the impostor tree is bad. Bad fruit is promoted by fake science, fear, and lies.

This revelation does not judge people. It only says which tree people are eating fruit from. The bad tree has the fruit of abortion on it. All the other fruit on that tree is not from God, like climate change.

God did not condemn Adam and Eve for eating from the forbidden fruit. He does not condemn anyone else for eating from the wrong tree either.

> *(John 3:17) For God did not send his Son into the world to condemn the world, but to save the world through him.*

God wants us to stop doing wrong things after we find out the truth. He forgives us for making mistakes. We simply ask him to forgive us, and He does.

God sent his Son to earth for a redo. Whoever believes in Jesus is promised eternal life. Jesus came and died on the cross to reverse course.

There are two births. One, we are born into our physical body as a baby. When we die, if we are blameless, we go to Heaven. That begins our second birth.

Who is blameless? All unborn and young children. All who claim in their heart Jesus is the Son of God are blameless too. He lives there invisibly.

Every person has a spirit. Our spirits which came from Heaven at conception can return to Heaven when we die.

Our soul goes with our spirit. Our soul is our mind, memories, and emotions. The impostor on earth tortures us by our mistakes. He constantly reminds us of them.

Our mistakes do not follow us around in Heaven. God, in his mercy, removes them as far as the east is from the west. In other words, they are completely removed out of our soul.

We get to choose if we go to Heaven or descend to Hell. We can reject or accept Jesus. Those that accept Jesus and keep him alive in their heart go to Heaven. It is risky to not make a decision. Not accepting Jesus is like rejecting Him.

There are also two deaths. First, our physical body dies. That is the first death. The second death is reserved for those who do not accept Jesus into their heart.

God gave Adam and Eve a warning. Eat from all trees but the forbidden one. They were conned by the wily serpent and did it anyway. People of today still eat from the bad tree.

That's why we need a Savior. Jesus died to take away our sin. We cannot save ourselves. Jesus took our place on the cross to prevent us from being tortured in Hell.

God gives us a promise. Believe in my Son and have eternal life.

(John 3:16) For God so loved the world that he gave his one and only Son, that whoever believes in him shall not perish but have eternal life.

It's a free gift from God to go to Heaven. Jesus paid for us. That's what makes it free. God knows we cannot do anything on our own to go there. Trying our best to be "good" is not enough.

God doesn't want us in Hell. It's a torture chamber. Demons cut people in two there. Then the spirit body returns to whole. Then it is cut in two again, and again. Unending agony awaits all whose name is not in the book of life.

God wants us returned to him. He grieves for us. He desires our affection. He loves us that much.

God sent his Son to be tortured in our place. It was horrible. First, he was whipped. It ripped open his flesh. Then he walked, carrying the heavy cross to the hill. It exhausted him, so he needed help carrying it.

Each walking step caused searing pain. Think of a paper cut. It stings when our finger moves pulling apart the healing skin.

Jesus had deep gashes all over his body. His ripped apart flesh hurt badly as he walked.

Later he was nailed to a cross. Spikes were driven through his wrists and ankles to hold him. Then he hung there, slowly suffocating. Jesus gladly did it to spare us eternal death. God loves us so much, he sent his Son to die in our place.

The story of the two moms gets very personal. We are that child. There is a tug-of-war going on for our soul. The devil seeks our everlasting destruction in Hell. God, represented by the real mom, wants us to live forever with him.

Wisdom came to rescue us. We are rescued from descending to Hell by Jesus if we choose him.

God loves everyone dearly. But only those without sin can enter Heaven. Jesus came to earth to die in our place. He forgives all our sins to cleanse our hearts.

Going to the devil's torturous prison is what happens to people if they do not have Jesus in their heart when they die.

The impostor spirit says there is no Hell. Who will people believe? God and his scripture? Or the impostor spirit promoting death?

Impostors desire the population to radically decrease. Abortion isn't doing enough. Sixty to seventy million less children in the United States since the Supreme Court decision in 1973 isn't decreasing world population.

The United States of America exports abortion to the rest of the world. We give our tax dollars as "foreign aid." It is funding global genocide.

Abortion figures outside the US are staggering. It makes our numbers tiny. Even with the horrid atrocities of abortion in place, impostors know they must do more things to reduce world population.

They desire to harm humans by creating sterility, cause reproductive issues, induce new things like autism, slap on long prison terms for minor crimes to lock up girls and boys during childbearing years, especially for minorities, and create gender confusion.

The common factor in all of the above is people caught in those circumstance will not produce children.

There is more. Dead people don't produce children either. Starvation, wars, disease, gang wars, drug overdose, and many other factors kill people. These are not random earthly happenings. Impostor elitists distress the world. Oppression of wars, disease, and starvation often occur in poor countries.

Third world countries are mostly kept poor. Impostor repression on them causes it. They stir up trouble to cause strife.

Impostors rely on false science to promote their claims. Flimsy paper face coverings or cute cloth designer masks stop nothing from spreading.

False science is a primary impostor ploy.

Any man with man relationship or woman with woman keeps those couples from creating babies.

Less babies on earth is important to them. Impostors always promote ways to decrease population.

Liar spirits cause confusion. Confusion creates feelings. Feelings are real. Why do I feel this way? Liar spirits cause the confusion, then a person is offered counterfeit solutions by more liar spirits.

It is one of the easiest science tests there is. Whatever the body parts under the clothing shows what the child was meant to be.

Impostors promote cloning. Belly bumps can be worn under garments for nine months to pretend a man is pregnant. Impostors desire to bypass the natural order laid forth from the beginning of God's creation to "go forth and multiply."

They want to prove creation can come from them, not God.

9

LOVE VS. HATE

Speaking harshly to someone who is different from us is not loving. Jesus was kind and gentle to the masses. He performed miracles. He spoke about the kingdom of Heaven and eternal life.

God sent Jesus not to condemn the world, but to save it through him.

Accusing someone is not how God wants us to be. Gossiping is not from God. He views it as very bad behavior.

> *(Proverbs 16:28) A perverse person stirs up conflict, and a gossip separates close friends.*

Here is some more. A gossip is listed in the group of very misfortunate company.

> *(Romans 1:29–31)... They are gossips, slanderers, God-haters, insolent, arrogant*

and boastful; they invent ways of doing evil; they disobey their parents; they have no understanding, no fidelity, no love, no mercy.

The impostor spirit loves when people bash each other. He loves it when we talk behind someone's back. The evil one craves dissension and hate. This includes perceived gender differences.

God loves humanity. He despises the devil. The evil one is destined to eternal death in Hell's lake of fire.

The devil doesn't believe it. He even lies to himself. He thinks he can still beat God by his trickery and deception. God isn't concerned. He is in control.

We do not stoop to the lows of mean behavior. We avoid saying unkind things to people who are different. And if we do it and realize it afterward, we simply say we are sorry.

The Lord is kind, patient, gentle, and loving. We strive to be like him and apologize to Him when we aren't.

10

THE INVITATION

We get to choose which Father we will spend eternity with. The Heavenly Father of joyous love, or the father of lies in Hell.

Impostor voices divide us. They divide us by skin color. And political party. They divide us by religion. They name some of us heterosexual, bisexual, and homosexual.

Despite all of this, people are more alike than different. Every one of us is a descendant of Adam and Eve. We are human. And because of our common ancestry, we will all die. The devil won death in the Garden of Eden.

Jesus came to rescue humanity. It is the same choice since he walked the earth. We accept Jesus into a heart, or not. It matters not the color of our skin. nor our gender.

If a person has not accepted Jesus into their heart and knows it, now is a good time to start a new beginning. Say something like the following example of a sinner's prayer.

Lord Jesus, I am sorry for my mistakes. Make me a new creation in you. Come into my heart. Guide me in the ways I should go. Amen.

Some people who, at one time, believed in God but no longer do, need to renew their vows. If the reader is not sure, go ahead and pray it.

A prayer like above is so easy. After saying it, a person is saved. God wipes away all of our past sin. We become pure. We join the blameless because of what Jesus did on the cross.

After we invite Jesus into our heart, he will never leave if we keep him alive there. We can get too busy and forget about him. We can start living a life without him. Then we are in trouble.

We must stay connected to him. Reading the bible is so very important. It may be helpful to get a children's bible for starters. Learn about the major characters and get an overview.

When beginning to read scripture, the book of John is a good place to start. Perhaps afterward, read Genesis and Exodus. The old and new testaments are closely connected.

There are online ministries. Many local churches post their messages spoken during worship meetings.

New followers of Jesus may want to listen to online or TV ministries for a while before attending a church in person.

Consider tuning into <u>In Touch Ministries.</u> Dr. Charles Stanley is a nationally respected bible-based minister. Local TV and cable channels carry his broadcast.

There are three forms of God. The Father, the Son Jesus, and the Spirit of God.

Each is the holy love of God in different form. It is like water having three characteristics (ice, liquid, steam or mist). All of it is water, but operates differently based upon the natural law of temperature.

A few years ago, at age seven, Josiah Cullen received an amazing revelation from the Lord. Learning to type on a special device to aid autistic children, he wrote simple to understand descriptors of the Trinity from God. Jump ahead to Chapter 25 if you'd like to review them now.

All three forms of God are love. On earth Jesus modeled His Father in Heaven. He died to set us free. When he went back home to Heaven to be with His Father, the Holy Spirit was sent to earth.

11

HIS GIFTS AND GREATER GIFTS

Before Jesus returned to Heaven, he told his friends (his closest followers) he would go away, but come back for them.

He is talking about bringing them to Heaven.

In His Father's house are many mansions. We'll be escorted to Heaven after our body dies if we have Jesus in our heart.

Jesus healed the sick, gave sight to the blind, gave hearing to the deaf, the lame walked, he cast out demons, and preached the good news of Heaven to everyone willing to listen.

He asked us to do the same and even more. Greater things he said we will do in his name. He was given all authority in Heaven and earth by His Father. Jesus allows us to operate in His authority.

Some congregations operate in many kinds of Holy Spirit gifts already. It is spreading. I'm convinced it will sweep through the American Church.

Jesus has many names. One is Good Shepherd. Another is Great Physician. He is known by that one because he performed miracles to heal.

God is already doing miraculous healings all over America. Stories are not reported by the news media. They hide truth.

One of God's current prophets said an over-the-counter cancer cure is coming. When it happens, know that it is from the Lord. Another of the Lord's current prophets said five major diseases will leave the earth.

The impostor message of free government health care is nothing of the sort. It costs Americans billions upon billions of dollars. God's healing is free. Not only that, it can do what medicines cannot. There are no ill side effects.

Medical techniques cannot do what God's power does. People in America are being lifted out of wheel-chairs to walk. Hallelujah!

Government is supposed to serve the people in a godly way, not to enslave people to trust the government for their food, shelter, and health care.

Impostors in government steal from people through taxation.

People are to fund the government. Scripture says so. But the same impostors who hate the unborn over-tax citizens by stealing much of it for their ungodly passions.

To those who knowingly promote evil as good, God's justice is coming. For the rest of us, the wisdom of Jesus is showing us his truths. Many who do not know the Lord will receive him.

Father God recreates us. He makes us new, over and over again, to fulfill his purpose. Amen. Come, Lord Jesus.

12

HOLY WISDOM

Wisdom gave the child back to the real mom of King Solomon's court.

What did the impostor mom desire? When wisdom exposed her, she wanted the child cut in two. She desired death.

She (the devil) fought for death in the Garden of Eden. She continues fighting for it to this day.

She fights for death of every unborn child in the womb. It's a custody battle.

She also fights for the eternal death of every living person. She desires we reject Jesus in this life.

Satan lies. The impostor mom spirit says there is no God. Or Jesus was a teacher, not the Savior. Or that there are multiple paths to Heaven.

All of that is lies. Scripture is very clear.

> *(John 14:6) Jesus answered, "I am the way and the truth and the life. No one comes to the Father except through me."*

The story of King Solomon's court battle is so much more than a story. With a few word substitutions, it is clear the story is about you and me.

Here are substitutions:

God (life or Heaven) = real mom.
Devil (death or Hell) = impostor mom.
Wisdom = Jesus.
Baby (you and me) = humanity.

Let's play it out. The impostor mom desires us, the baby, cut in two. The real mom wants us whole. God is the real mom. He wants us to enjoy an incredible life with him in Heaven.

He sent wisdom to save the baby (us). Wisdom is Jesus. God sent Jesus to rescue us from death in Hell.

The interesting thing is we get to choose. We have free will. We can believe Jesus was sent to save us and give us eternal life in Heaven.

Or we can believe the liar impostor. We can reject wisdom and spend eternity in the devil's pit.

It's an awful place. It's hideous. Torturous. Pain and suffering there is beyond belief.

Isolated spirits everywhere in the darkness holler in agony. Spirit bodies feel the torture. Shrieking pierces ears. The putrid odors wreak in that place. Every sense the person has is in Hell. The tongue longs for even a drop of water. Thirst is unquenchable. Scripture confirms this.

The stakes are high.

What will each person on earth do? Believe the father of lies and descend to Hell?

Or accept Jesus in one's heart and receive the promise of eternal life? We can be born into the heavenly realm. Joy, love, peace and comfort abound. No sickness, pain, sorrow, or sin is there.

Jesus takes our sin away. He makes us white as snow. We are pure.

No sin is allowed in Heaven. Unless a person repents of sin and accepts Jesus, they cannot enter.

> *(John 8:24) I told you that you would die*
> *in your sins; if you do not believe that I*
> *am he, you will indeed die in your sins.*

Some say if God doesn't accept everyone, who wants a God like that? It's so sad. They have made their choice.

Believe lies. Believe God. We get to choose. We accept wisdom or reject it.

The King Solomon court case is wisdom speaking into this age. It is wisdom to defeat abortion. And it is also wisdom to defeat death of our soul and spirit.

Glory to you, O Lord, for your wisdom. The name above all names did the unthinkable to conquer death.

Like that rock that toppled Goliath, the devil didn't see it coming. The devil wanted earth to himself. He thought killing Jesus would do it.

It was the opposite. It sealed his eternal fate in the lake of fire.

Jesus won victory over death. He and Father God did their part. Now it is up to us to accept that victory for our eternal life. If not saved, consider the prayer below.

Come Lord Jesus. Forgive my past mistakes. Make me pure. Enter my heart to be my Savior. I choose you. Lead my life. Keep me on the right path. Amen.

The impostor mom story defeats abortion.

It contains wisdom leading to eternal life in Heaven if people so choose.

It is also prophecy. The story foretold Jesus's coming to earth a thousand years before his birth. Humanity was stolen from God in the Garden of Eden. Then Jesus comes to give humanity back to its rightful parent—God.

So much of scripture is hidden prophecy. It's like when Jesus said destroy this temple and I'll raise it up in three days. He was talking about His death and resurrection. People thought he meant Solomon's temple.

When Jesus spoke of eunuchs, I believe it was prophecy too.

In ancient days a man's body was purposely maimed against his will so he could not father children. Eunuchs were put in charge of a King's harem. Kings couldn't trust someone to supervise all their wives who could produce offspring.

(Matthew 19:11–12) Jesus replied, "Not everyone can accept this word, but only those to whom it has been given. For there are eunuchs who were born that way, and there are eunuchs who have been made eunuchs by others—and there are those who choose to live like eunuchs for the sake of the kingdom of heaven. The one who can accept this should accept it."

Jesus said there are three types of eunuchs. One kind are the physically altered ones. They were men whose body was changed by force.

The second type are those choosing not to unite with a woman. Or a woman choosing not to unite with a man. They make lifetime vows of service to the Lord. They made decisions not to marry or have sex.

There is the third type. Jesus said those that can accept it should accept it. To me this is Jesus speaking about himself.

God is spirit. God has no sexual desire because he has no physical body.

Jesus is born holy. He said he can only do what His Father says or does in Heaven. Jesus has no sexual desire because His Father in Heaven has none.

He has the parts of a man, but won't use them to procreate. The children he gives His Father are in spirit. Any person on earth who accepts Jesus as their Savior becomes a child of God.

Scripture says in Heaven, we are not given in marriage. In Heaven we become so holy we have no sexual desire. All who are reborn into Heaven become eunuchs like Jesus.

Jesus said some are born eunuchs. It's plural. That means if he is one, then there is at least one more. I suspect he was talking about his relative, John the Baptist.

> *(Matthew 11:11) Truly I tell you, among those born of women there has not risen anyone greater than John the Baptist; yet whoever is least in the kingdom of heaven is greater than he.*

Jesus said John was the greatest man ever to be born of a woman. Jesus the Messiah was born holy. John was next born holy. Listen in when John's dad was visited by the same angel as Jesus's mom, Mary.

> *(Luke 1:15–17) For he will be great in the sight of the Lord. He is never to take wine or other fermented drink, and he will be filled with the Holy Spirit even before he is born. He will bring back many of the people of Israel to the Lord their God. And he will go on before the Lord, in the spirit and power of Elijah, to turn the hearts of the parents to their children and the disobedient to the wisdom*

of the righteous—to make ready a people
prepared for the Lord.

John is filled with the Holy Spirit even before birth. He has an earthly role to prepare hearts for Jesus.

Both boys were named by God. Also, both were born holy after holy conceptions. John's mom was too old to have a child. The angel Gabriel said to Mary, who was a virgin, all things are possible for God.

Now back to summarize the three types of eunuchs. The first type is physically altered, so they cannot procreate by sex. Then there are those who choose not to have sex to honor the Holy Father with their life. And finally, those so Holy, they were born with no sexual desire.

Impostors claim Jesus's story about eunuchs prove gender confused are born that way. That's illogical. But impostors put forth illogical thought and get people to buy in.

In contrast to Jesus, the evil one teaches us to have corrupt sex. He tempts us with sex before marriage, have sex with ourselves, commit sex with someone other than our spouse, or with someone of the same sex.

Impostors point out our differences. Yet we are more alike than different. Each individual gets the same choice. Accept or reject Jesus.

Impostor promoters have steered us to believe their nonsense. This is not viewed well from Heaven.

Jesus came to rescue us. It explains this book's title, *Rescue Us Wisdom*. We cannot rescue ourselves. Without Jesus, we are destined to Hell when we die.

The devil provides busyness and distractions to keep people from finding or seeking Jesus. Then he is happy to take those individuals to Hell, subjecting them to unending torture.

Believe God, or believe the liar.

We can learn another thing from King Solomon's court. The devil stole God's humanity when it was young. That's an operational strategy of the devil. Steal from God when something is new.

Christians left England for America to escape persecution. When our country was young, the early settlers and indigenous peoples coexisted.

After the initial colony became established the impostor spirit showed up. Human slaves were brought here.

At some point the impostor spirit began dehumanizing native tribes. They were called heathens and savages. It happened while America was still young. Many from the existing nations perished.

Their lands were taken. Treaties were bungled and broken. The trail of tears and other atrocities produced hardship and death.

The impostor spirit of World War Two hated the Jews, but even more than just them. And, anyone in occupied lands who stood up against tyranny was rounded up and shot.

The impostor spirit hates all classes of Americans. Their hatred is fiercest toward minorities. At much higher percentages, their babies die by abortion. Some are lost in gang fights. Some are locked up for long prison terms during their childbearing years. A high percentage are kept poor. They are taught to trust government rather than God for what they need.

The impostor spirit is a liar.

The impostor spirit steals, kills, and destroys.

Impostors termed US indigenous people savages and heathens. Impostors don't do the dirty work themselves. They convince others to do it for them.

From the cross Jesus said, forgive them Father, for they know not what they do. Jesus meant that for everyone. Even impostors.

Apostle Paul thought he was doing God's work too. His name was Saul at the time. He put early Christians in jail, had them beat, and killed some. Terrorists in many countries still do that.

Saul encountered Jesus on the road to Damascus. His story is in the book of Acts.

Then the Lord gave Saul the name Paul with a new life. He became mighty for God. He switched sides.

What happened to Saul still happens today. People who are taught to hate followers of Jesus have dreams or visions. They encounter Him. Then they switch sides to follow Jesus.

God made Paul his instrument of love. He does the same for all who receive him.

Many who convicted Jesus to die on the cross repented. God, through Jesus, redeemed them. That story is also in the New Testament book of Acts.

Nothing changes under the sun. The way the devil operates is the same as in the beginning.

President Lincoln was against slavery. Freedoms were won by the hand-to-hand combat of the American Civil War. But then impostors reinvented slavery in a new way. They enslaved the same class of people, and more, by Hate Trap techniques. Those opposed to abortion are termed haters, Nazis, and worse. It's a relentless barrage of lies to make lies appear as truth.

They lie like the impostor mom in King Solomon's court. She accuses the real mom of being the liar and the evil thief.

Vote the impostors out of government. Stop giving the impostor political party power with votes.

Judges who once were on the side of abortion can repent. Judges and politicians that defy wisdom to continue protecting abortion and all impostor fruit will harm themselves.

Impostors who steal God's rainbow as a sign of their own will no longer be able to steal elections.

Impostors, given no authority by God, work tirelessly to steal it from people. People give their authority to impostors by voting for them.

Saying all the above doesn't make republican politicians truthful. Many national and state republican government officials secretly work with the impostor spirit. They are republicans in name only. The republican party has been infiltrated. Self-interest, not the people's interest, dominates their agendas. They stifle attempts of honest people to expose impostor schemes.

National officials and some at state level on both sides of the aisle stuff their pockets with bribes, kickbacks, power, and prestige. Others comply because of threats.

Do impostors who use worldly tactics think their actions go unnoticed in Heaven?

Americans need to wise up. Americans must become the nation God intended it to be before the impostor spirit infiltrated. It happened when our nation was young.

The news media participates. They actively promote impostor agenda. The bad fruit is made into good. The good fruit is made into bad. They call evil good and good evil.

> *(Isaiah 5:20) Woe to those who call evil good and good evil, who put darkness for light and light for darkness, who put bitter for sweet and sweet for bitter.*

Public school systems have a lot of explaining to do. Indoctrinating very young kids in theories and sexual orientations confuses kids. Does God condone this? Impostors lie. There are only two genders.

"Higher" education professors in certain classes at colleges and universities assault Christian students' faith. The higher-ups there—including deans, board of regents, chancellors, and presidents—permit it to happen.

It's time to repent.

> *(Matthew 18:6) If anyone causes one of these little ones—those who believe in me—to stumble, it would be better for them to have a large millstone hung around their neck and to be drowned in the depths of the sea.*

Television, music, movies, cartoons, and other "programming" from media sources do impostor work too. Symbolism is flashed about and embedded in their episodes to openly laugh at napping Americans.

Research pedophilia. Afterward, look for their pedophilia symbols in logos. It's sickening.

They put their signature on it right under the sleeping public's nose. Child abduction is big business. Global networks rake in trillions.

Being paid handsomely the entertainment industry pushes impostor agendas. Advertisers join right in. They pedal the impostor filth for profit too.

The church is divided. Impostor thought has entered. It is time for clergy to stop listening to voice of man. Members complain about all kinds of things.

Clergy respond to it. We are to fear the Lord, not people.

God loves his shepherds. His correction is not meant to harm, but to change hearts. Liberal social agendas must exit the church.

Scripture says we cannot be at His table taking communion while also drinking at the table of abortion and the other bad fruit on that same tree.

> *(1 Corinthians 10:21) You cannot drink the cup of the Lord and the cup of demons too; you cannot have a part in both the Lord's table and the table of demons.*

Certainly, God wants his good news preached. Bending the gospel to adapt to culture must end. God is looking for shepherds to accept wisdom from King Solomon's court.

A new wave of power from Heaven is coming. Congregations can operate in power and authority to heal, perform miracles, practice deliverance, and usher in the even greater things Jesus promised.

All of this is for God's glory. Not our glory to say, look at my congregation, or look what I am doing as a shepherd of my church.

No, God wants people to think, I go there because God is there. I want to worship the Lord there because his presence is there.

To be greatest of all, Jesus said we become servant to all.

The religious sects of Jesus's time were against God, not for him. They persecuted Jesus because he was Lord of the Sabbath. Jesus healed on Sunday, but the religious leaders objected. They considered it breaking God's law.

Some religious leaders were jealous of Jesus. They desired to be exalted by the peoples, and he was taking the spotlight off of them.

They accused him of serious other offenses because they did not know him.

Some clergy today are so opposed to healing they teach it is from the devil.

It is true the devil can imitate God. There is no such thing as a "good" witch. Witches will deceptively "heal" people. Learn to discern correctly. God is going to release all kinds of heavenly gifts. Ask to receive. Knock and it will be opened.

Jesus healed on the Sabbath. So can congregations.

Molly White authored a book titled *Deceived: God Brought Purpose From My Pain*. Congregations can benefit from understanding what happened to millions of women and men. Losing their unborn children to impostor lies harmed them deeply.

Congregations can contribute to emotional healing by conducting memorial services for the unborn. Molly offers more useful ideas on pages 149–151 of her book.

13

PAGAN INFLUENCE

In America, our days of the week and months are named after pagan gods and pagan rulers. Why? Does this please God? Why doesn't anyone notice?

Why are all those gods taught in public school, but the one true God is not?

Who sets the agenda of public schools? God? Not by a far cry. Why? The impostor spirit has grown strong in America.

Our calendar reveres Roman pagan gods. The names of the week bow to them. Monthly names honor Roman pagan gods and Roman pagan emperors.

The days of the week should be renamed to remember God and what he has done for humanity. It is the opposite right now. Our calendar is structured to remember false gods.

The seven days of the week can be turned away from pagan gods to our creator God. Names can parallel the seven days of creation.

Day seven, when God rested, becomes Son Day, replacing Sunday. We are an English-speaking nation. English terms make it easy for kids to learn the meanings.

Son Day is more appropriate for the last day of the week than as the first day. The Sabbath Day is represented by the seventh day of creation.

Day six, when animals were created, seems appropriate to be named Lamb Day. Jesus is the Lamb of God.

On the first day of creation came light. Jesus is the light of the world. It seems appropriate to replace the pagan name Monday with Light Day.

Tuesday, the second day, gives way to Sky Day.

Wednesday, the third day, perhaps can become Tree Day. Jesus is the Tree of Life. The cross he hung on is referred to as a tree. The fruit on his tree produces life.

A suggestion for Thursday is Sign Day. The stars and moon were created in the Heavens as markers. God shows us timetables for events by these lights.

Day five, replacing Friday, can become Fish Day. A fish is an early Christian symbol. It reminds us of the scripture. Four of the twelve apostles were fisherman by trade. Jesus said to Peter, I will teach you to be a fisher of men. All of this can be reminders to us on Fish Day.

Months can be renamed to the twelve stones of the book of Revelation. In obedience we honor God in America, not pagans.

What has happened to America's holidays? Holiday is short for holy day. Is Halloween holy? It is a day to honor witches, vampires, and wearing masks. Wearing masks is not who God created us to be.

Some wear a mask of pretend self. They don't think their real self will be appealing to attract friends. So they pretend to be someone else.

Some boys pretend to love with a mask of affection to steal a girl's body for their pleasure.

Boys will be boys is a lie. Boys are taught ungodly behavior by impostor voices of this world. This must change.

Boys must become gentlemen like of old.

Some hide behind a mask of alcohol or drugs. The world teaches that these bring joy and acceptance. It's a false message. They can quickly turn addictive.

The impostor desires we wear masks of self-indulgence. That means serve our own self. Buy this and be happy. Do this and be happy. Wear this and be happy. To be accepted by people, do this or that.

In these above examples we find the impostor spirit coaxing us to wear masks.

Some find perverse pleasure in pictures or videos posted by sex promoters. Buying images is the biggest industry in America. Curiosity can lead to total control. Morning, noon, and night, people search and watch. Alluring temptation pulls them in.

America is caught in the bondage of sexual sin. Online sites rake in trillions. Porn and smut sell. It is poisoning souls.

This giant must fall. Come, Lord Jesus, slay this monster. Cleanse us and reduce to dust this evil sexual empire imprisoning our nation's populace.

Lord, rescue those caught in sin's addictive snare. Say, *Lord, I have sinned. Rescue me Jesus. Break the yoke of_____ off of me. Cleanse me. Make me a new creation in you. Amen.*

Fill in the blank. It could be porn. It could be alcohol or drugs. It could be adultery. It could be gambling. There are many addictions.

Ask the Lord to be rescued. How he does it is up to Him. He is faithful and trustworthy.

Prostitution and sex trafficking of women and children must end. Evil people lock them in cages, then dupe people to have sex with them or sell them at the going price. Wake up, America. Speak up. Cry out for these lost ones who deserve a new life in Messiah Jesus. Rescue them.

Impostors say speaking out about a certain sexual sin is hate speech. In Canada, it is now a law. Speak against homosexuality, and you can be arrested and imprisoned.

Impostors have erected laws in the US to keep gender confused children from getting the help they need.

People do leave homosexual lifestyles. Then the ones celebrating a person's coming out become hostile and persecute them. If it's such a healthy lifestyle, why must promoters heap hate on someone who leaves it?

These same impostors protect the porn industry as free speech. They allow flag burning. They allow burning down cities under the pretense of racial justice.

Minority business owners lost family businesses. Places to shop for groceries or other products were torched. Many without vehicles must now go further for basic needs.

Hate pretends to be love. It is shocking how many Americans fall for it.

(Proverbs 29:7) The righteous care about justice for the poor, but the wicked have no such concern.

Impostors have great control of thought. The above examples illustrate the point.

They get us to pay them money for what causes self-destruction. Imagine the political donations that city burning across the nation produced.

Thank God for his forgiveness. We need his mercy for what we have done, and his grace for what we are unable to do.

14

FAITH IS PICTURE IT DONE

Josiah Cullen says faith is picture it done.

Picture it done: abortion falls. Lord, end the American Civil War Against Humanity. We praise you, Jesus, for the victory! Giants do fall.

Picture it done: post-abortive moms and dads have their broken hearts restored. Come, Holy Spirit, come. Restore souls. Replace sorrow with your Spirit, bringing comfort and joy.

Many will come to the Lord because of what happened to their child. Hallelujah! Their children whom they've never met will beckon them from Heaven to come live there.

Many, many will! Praise God!

What the impostor intended for harm God turns to joy for those who love Him. They will be reunited with their unborn children in Heaven.

Picture it done: the porn industry falls. Come, Host from Heaven. By the power of Jesus, crush darkness.

Picture it done: racial injustice ends. The pleas of the poor are valid. Bring your justice, Father.

Picture it done: financial independence comes to all. Let the body of the Lord be their help and not the false god government.

Reclaim your cherished peoples, Lord. Sever the grip of the oppressors. Be a lamp unto the feet of the oppressed. Lead them to your victory in Christ Jesus.

Lord Jesus, stand and calm the storm in our cities. Impostors have orchestrated urban destruction. Bring your peace and justice, Lord.

Picture it done: our nation repents and becomes a Godly nation, worshipping the Almighty God. Let us give Him honor, glory, praise, and adoration for his loving kindness and promises of life in the full.

Be bound in your own chains, Satan.

America has tried it her way. Return to the Lord, the giver of light, truth, and the way.

Join hands, urban, suburban, and rural Americans. Unite in the Lord our God. Vote in primary elections. Too many established infiltrators remain. Then vote in state and national elections.

In all ways, honor the Sabbath, not going our own way. Employers, end policies forcing workers to work on Son Day, or else be fired. Construct policies to honor the Lord.

If an essential service, such as clergy, health services, fire, police, and similar functions, provide a suitable different day for them to pay homage to the Lord.

Many businesses and sports franchises should simply close for the day. They infringe upon the Lord's day. They can work six days a week and rest on the Sabbath.

Sport teams survived a whole year without admission sales. Why must they gouge attendees with greedy entry, food, and beverage prices? Are expensive gate prices and concessions to restrict the poor from attending? They have explaining to do.

Individuals, too, should honor the Lord on his day. Is God our God? How are individuals showing it?

Picture it done: the educational system kindergarten through college/university, all levels, turn away from indoctrinating falsehoods into children. Lord, turn these into holy institutions of your knowledge and truths.

Picture it done: the motion picture industry turns from its violent representation of modern life. They put forth darkness for light. Let their night turn to dawn. Thank you, Lord Jesus.

Picture it done: the media industry turns godly. Censorship and fake news must end.

They are exposed by their stance toward abortion. Prolife marchers in Washington, DC, of thousands upon thousands are given scant coverage. But media falls all over themselves to celebrate women's reproductive "rights." Media glorifies death.

Impostors give trophies and awards to famous abortion promoters. Rescue us, Lord.

God's children must not wag or point fingers at others. Instead, learn to point at the Lord above. Be like him. Point to his love, mercy, grace, and forgiveness. Be kind and gentle. Be welcoming.

Jesus wasn't tolerant. He turned over the money changer tables in the temple. He drove them out with a whip.

We are not to tolerate darkness. Speak. Use your voice. Vote. Teach children correctly about God and Jesus that they are love, light, and merciful. Unify with other believers. Hold impostor companies accountable. Boycott them. Money is their language.

Jesus makes us clean. Nothing we can do will save us. We can't earn Heaven. Jesus is the only one who can open the door to Heaven for us. And it's a free gift. He paid for us.

15

COMPASSIONATE JESUS

Jesus spoke a new command. Love your neighbor as ourselves. He is kind and gentle. Lean into Him. We leave our burdens at his feet, and he makes our yoke light.

There is a story which Jesus told to illustrate being neighborly.

A man was traveling by himself. Thieves beat him and stole what he had. He lay half dead at the side of the road.

Remember, in Jesus's day, people traveled by walking or perhaps on a donkey, camel, or horse.

Two travelers passed by the dying man, but did not involve themselves.

Then came the good Samaritan. He ministered to the lifeless person on the spot. Then he brought the man to a place for care. He stayed overnight with him at an inn, paying the price himself. When he went away the next day, he said he'd return and repay any cost for nursing this person back to life.

I'm convinced this good Samaritan is a parable about Jesus himself.

Let's observe Jesus in action today.

The impostor spirit of abortion steals her baby and shatters her heart. The destroyer left her half dead along the road of life. She was lied to. She believed her life would go back to "normal." Instead, her soul is ripped to shreds.

It gets worse. The impostor spirit abuses her. He accuses and blames—look what you did to your child. Then piles on more lies—God will never forgive you for what you've done.

The devil caused her abortion. He lied. Then heaps punishment on her for what <u>he</u> did. He blames her. The devil does not own up to his wickedness. He lies even to himself.

(Psalm 109:16) For he never thought of doing a kindness, but hounded to death the poor and the needy and the brokenhearted.

Jesus shows up after the impostor did his dirty work. He lifts her and carries her to a safe place. He nurtures her back to life.

Jesus loves her. He forgives her. He gives her a new heart to replace the one broken into a thousand pieces.

(Psalm 34:18) The Lord is close to the brokenhearted and saves those who are crushed in spirit.

God adopted her child. Her baby is in Heaven. She will be united with her child forever, if she dies on earth with Jesus in her heart. What the devil intended for evil, God turns to good for those who love him.

That's the peace that passes all understanding. She got duped into making a mistake. God, in his mercy, by his Son's passion for us, redeems us for eternity.

Jesus died not only for our salvation. He died to remove our emotional suffering.

That's holy love.

Jesus is the good Samaritan. It happens on the road of life. The thief robs and beats us. We are left for dead. Then Jesus comes. He takes us to a place of recovery. On the cross, He paid for us. He restores us in this life.

He went away to Heaven. One day he will return to bring his believers there. In Heaven he gives rewards for believers who did his loving work on earth.

The good Samaritan story has infinite variations. Many things leave us half dead on the side of the road. Jesus shows up to restore us.

There's another story about a woman who is at a dinner Jesus was invited to attend.

She is weeping. Her tears moisten his dusty feet. They are soiled from walking outdoors on the dirt roads.

She wipes them clean with her long hair. Then she pours perfume on them.

This woman is frowned upon by the host of the dinner. She has a wayward occupation. It's unclean. The host is appalled at Jesus's willingness to let her touch him.

This woman silently dropped tears of sorrow on Him. Her shame is poured out. In response, Jesus wraps her with his love and forgiveness.

He said to her, your faith has saved you.

In that moment did he declare that surely goodness and mercy shall follow you all the days of your life? Didn't he also, in that instant, promise her she would live in the house of the Lord forever?

Wasn't she at the table of her enemies? The ones that scorn her do not want Jesus touching her.

She covered His feet with perfume. Did He respond by anointing her head, in the spirit, with oil?

There are lessons to learn. We avoid acting like the host of that meal. Grace replaces judgment. We love the ones seeking Jesus.

We all desire mercy, forgiveness, and grace. Because he first loved us, we welcome all into the Lord's house.

Pastors and congregations can benefit from a book study discussion of *Words That Work*, written by Cindy McGill.

We become like Jesus, the friend of sinners. He loves them. We are friendly, kind, and welcoming like him. Parishioners can be harshly judgmental. Instead, we minister like the compassionate Jesus.

She had sexual sins. Who in America doesn't? Adultery is sin. Self-gratification is sin. Sex before marriage is a sin. Lust is sin. Must I go on?

She had to overcome her fear of scorn to come to Jesus. Make it easy for those who feel just like her to find Jesus.

Here's another example.

Jesus met a woman at the ancient well of Jacob. It was a divine appointment. He came from Heaven to earth and then took a detour to go through Samaria.

It was intentional. There they met. She is alone. No friends. No family. He tells her to fetch her husband, but she replies, I have none.

Then he answers, you have spoken truthfully. The one you now have is not your husband, and you have had five previously. To Jesus, this did not matter.

He came to her. He offered her his living water that bubbles up to eternal life. She left her water jar at the well and went back to town. Have I found the Messiah? Come and see!

He comes to us too. Our past does not matter. He loves us all. He is eager to forgive us and make us a new creation in Him.

The impostor spirit says we are unworthy of God's love. The impostor is a liar. It is exactly the opposite. Jesus loved her. Is she the first evangelist? Many from her town believed in him because of her testimony.

Then they believe all the more because they met him themselves.

He rescued her. Then her words as a witness rescued others. That's how it happens. They came to him because of her.

There is another story. A woman was caught in adultery. Her punishment is to be death. She knows this. It is a well-known law back in Jesus's day.

Rocks will be hurled at her. Trauma will extinguish her breath.

When the irate mob seized her, she gave up hope. There is no escape. She is to die. Yet something remarkable happened. An intervention occurred.

The angry bunch brought her to Jesus. They want him to confirm the law of Moses. Surprisingly, he doesn't. Instead, he gently disperses the mob. He says whoever is without sin may throw the first stone.

His words stun them. It likely took a few moments of silence for his words to take hold. Then the oldest of the group began dropping their stones and walking away. One by one, the others followed.

Now alone with Jesus he speaks to her. Where are your accusers? She replies, she has none. He said, neither do I accuse you. Go and sin no more.

Learn from Jesus. Some say God is just waiting for us to make a mistake. Then he'll strike us down. That's a lie. If Jesus pardoned her, it is because His Father in Heaven desired it.

The impostor spirit lies. He lies about God's nature. It is the impostor devil who hates us. He is the one condemning people. The hateful devil yearns to hurl that first stone of death at us full force.

God is not like that. He sent his Son to die for us. Every one of us is that woman. Jesus redeems our life too. Then asks us to sin no more.

We slip. We make mistakes. Confess them and ask for forgiveness. As often as we ask in remorse, He forgives. Always.

She made a sexual mistake. Who in America hasn't?

If a man looks at a woman lustfully, Jesus says we have committed adultery in our hearts. James in his book says if we break a minor point of one law, we break them all.

Look at a woman lustfully one time in our life, and we break every law including murder. Sobering.

(1 John 1:8) If we claim to be without sin, we deceive ourselves and the truth is not in us.

We need forgiveness. We need mercy. We need grace. Jesus offers it all for free. That is good news indeed.

Whatever we've done in our past, hear and believe what Jesus spoke from the cross. Father, forgive them— they know not what they do. It is our hope. Cling to it.

Barabbas was to be put on the cross with the two thieves. It was the custom to release one prisoner during the Passover celebration. The Roman ruler Pontius Pilate was willing to release Jesus.

Instead, the impostor spirit whipped up the crowd to shout crucify Jesus. Barabbas was let go free. The innocent Jesus was condemned.

Barabbas had quite a rap sheet. He deserved death. Jesus took his place. Barabbas was set free.

We are all like Barabbas. Jesus died in our place too. By His blood, we can be forgiven. Then we become free too.

Receive Him. It is a free gift.

16

AMERICAN HOLIDAYS

In America, it is time to make holidays holy.

Halloween was originally All Saints Day. Impostor spirit hijacked it. No longer should it be about impostor symbolism and dark entities. We stop decorating our homes with their objects.

We also stop dressing our children or ourselves in their garb. The biggest trick of Halloween is it celebrates impostor darkness.

Impostors make their temptations fun. They make sin alluring. They fool us to celebrate their yuck.

Let's make All Saints Day fun and celebratory, but refocus it once again about God's saints. We commend them, but avoid worshipping them. Only God is to be worshipped.

Can't followers of the Lord design a holy day even more fun for kids than the dark side? Candy can stay. Fun can stay. The day is made super exciting.

Perhaps it is moved from outdoors to church buildings. Play games. Eat treats. Let children take candy home.

Learn about the saints. Maybe adults dress in costumes of saints. Teach kids about the different crowns in Heaven saints are given. Maybe kids get to bring home a crown.

Christmas was moved to the present timing for certain reasons by the church. Those reasons are no longer valid.

A pagan figure has replaced the real St. Nickolas. Commercialization has caused focus on Jesus to fracture.

St. Nickolas was a real man, and no, he didn't live at the North Pole. He didn't fly in a sleigh pulled by flying reindeer.

He lived hundreds of years ago. Nickolas was known for secretly giving gifts to needy children. Those are qualities to remember and cherish.

Honoring Saint Nickolas can be aligned to his established day—December sixth.

Eventually, kids discover who really gives the gifts. Then the accurate story of the real St. Nick can be told.

It can be just as much fun as today. Perhaps it becomes way less commercialized. Some children get too many presents. Emphasize St. Nicholas focused on giving gifts to the less fortunate. Kids can participate to help give gifts to others.

Appropriate focus includes charitable organization assistance to bless kids of families needing help.

Why should St. Nick and Jesus share the same day? Jesus deserves his own very special day. Historians can estimate which month he was born.

If America chooses the date to always fall on what today is Monday, then we'd celebrate his birthday on Light Day. He is the light that came into the world. It would be known as Christmas Light Day.

Christmas Eve would always be on Son Day. How symbolically special.

One fun tradition is baking a birthday cake for him and letting the wind outdoors blow out the candles. Sing happy birthday. Make it a holy and fun day.

There is worship time and singing familiar hymns and praise songs. The Lord cherishes his family singing to him.

Candy canes and chocolate, cookies and goodies—make it festive.

Write out birthday cards for Him. He will receive them as a delightful gift.

Jesus deserves his own day.

Easter is a pagan term having ties to pagan symbolism. It's time to rename the day. Some have already accurately replaced the pagan word Easter with Resurrection Day.

Eggs and rabbits are pagan symbols.

Kids can have just as much fun with candy shapes honoring the Lord. Christian symbols include the cross, a fish, and a lamb, among others.

The Sabbath is the last day of the week. Son Day replaces Sunday. The first day of the week becomes Light Day in place of Monday.

In future America, do we celebrate Jesus's resurrection on Resurrection Light Day, the first day of the week? It seems appropriate.

Praise and honor are yours, O Lord.

Valentine's Day celebrates cupid, a pagan sex god. It's a wonderful thought to give a special blessing to loved ones on a certain day of the year.

Cupid must go.

Consider a paradigm shift. Inside the card is a bible verse. Small changes can make it holy.

Write cards of love for the Father, and the Son, and the Holy Spirit. The Holy Spirit, I'm told, has a sense of humor. Give him some funny ones because he is such a "card." Ha-ha.

Kat Kerr has revealed that Jesus loves candy, flowers, and dancing. Father God has a unicorn. Rainbows of love pulsate joyously from Him. The Father loves teal blue and peacock feathers. These ideas help celebrate the day.

Send cards also to loved ones. Use bible verses. Candy, cards, flowers, hugs, and kisses all belong. Make it fun.

The tooth fairy is not a holiday, but can go.

<u>Saint Patrick</u> was a real man who evangelized Ireland. Commending him has given way to leprechauns and folklore. Celebrating Saint Patrick's Day needs to be rethought, at least in America.

It's not helpful for kids to believe in something and then learn it isn't real. There are too many kids that believe in God, but then stop. Learning Santa Claus, the Easter Bunny, Leprechauns, and the Tooth Fairy are all make-believe have negative impact. Kids can reason God is myth too.

The pagan ties to holidays can stop.

17

CORRECTIONS AND EXPOSURE

There are major monuments on our land erected by impostors. One of them was named after our first president. Its pyramid-shaped top is not a godly shape. It gives reverence to an ancient false god. It is like our enemy planted his flag on our land.

Our stately government buildings are in Roman architecture. Our schools teach about Roman gods. Our taxation system is designed like Roman times. It greatly oppresses us. Our calendar gives homage to Roman gods. America even has coliseums. Why all this Roman pagan influence?

These things do not glorify the Father. Jesus loves when our country glorifies him and His Father. Holy Spirit, help us as a nation to obliterate all Roman pagan trappings, even their Roman numerals.

A structure in Georgia lists ten false doctrines. One of the ten is to maintain earthly population at a fraction of today's population.

Then there is the "freedom" arch transported around the globe. It represents freedom from God at New World Order celebrations. It has been on American soil. Global elitists come. They embrace its ungodliness with satanic worship.

It is fitting and proper to grind these to dust and incinerate all remnant. Picture it done!

Undoubtedly, more structures need to come down.

There is an unfinished monument in South Dakota of Chief Crazy Horse on his horse. It can be completed with private donations. Perhaps the owners would consider donating it afterward to the National Park Service.

Crazy Horse on his horse should be remembered like the nearby four presidents.

Perhaps Dr. Martin Luther King Day can be renamed to Reverend or Pastor Martin Luther King Day. He was a godly man. It is a subtle change, but one that recognizes his love of the Lord.

The impostor spirit puts symbols right out in the open. Six-six-six is one of them, hidden in their logos.

Some also incorporate three-three or three-three-three. One-third of the angels were cast to earth due to disobedience. Secret dark societies use the three-threes symbolism.

Pedophilia symbols abound hidden in television shows, on participants' social media pages, and all about.

Some business logos incorporate a pedophilia four-color scheme.

Pizza and hot dog symbols represent pedophilia too. Disgustingly, the shape is the symbol. Think "V" shaped pizza pieces. Think of the shape of the hot dog. These are anatomy references of little children.

Advertisers of the trafficked use these codes. Buyers understand what is offered and at what price.

The V-shape and male-shape logos are out there. Companies have a lot of explaining to do. V is not the only impostor linked letter used.

Some apparel logos pay tribute to pagan gods. Parents are unaware. They "brand" their kids paying high prices to companies for it.

The five-point star has been stolen by impostors. A circle around it touching the five points is Satanist symbology. It's their worship circle. The star symbol with or without the circle is on about everything including military equipment.

Goat heads with horns and goat heads on a man's human body with a woman's chest are other symbols.

There is so much more.

Corporations shake hands with impostor plans. Does this go unnoticed in Heaven? Which companies silence free speech? Why all those extra unnecessary ingredients in food and drinks? What is hidden in artificial and natural ingredients?

Why are lawns and farm fields sprayed with toxins?

Who instituted tiling agricultural land?

Sediment and fertilizer drain into streams, county ditches, and rivers. Waters pristine a hundred years ago are murky brown. Silt covers what was sand, rock, and pebbles. Fish are unhealthy to eat.

Lakes fill with fertilizers, too, from rain and snow runoff.

What is hidden in medicines? Why are extreme side effects permitted? Do nonprofits steal money? Do they and foundations advertise for good, but use funds to advance harm?

Why do some jets in the sky produce long lasting white streaks while others do not?

Is ground beef, pork, sausage, and pepperoni mixed with disgusting impurities?

Why does ice cream have natural and artificial ingredients? Home recipes taste great without them. Why are they added to most foods and beverages? What is hidden in artificial and natural ingredients?

What harm do birth control pills cause? Is fooling a body to believe it is pregnant for years healthy? Who says? Aren't the same people promoting abortion?

Question everything. Impostor elites steal, kill, and destroy. They desire control. Their freedom is freedom from God. Our downfall has been plotted by these elites for eons. Unknowingly, people comply. Doing what they want us to do becomes social norms.

Knowingly, impostor elites plot it all. Their most loyal minions gladly play along. They are promised wealth, or power, or both. Others join in due to black-mail, threats, or other types of underworld pressure.

Unknowingly, many Americans support impostors because of repeated lies. Repeated lies cause confusion. The ones believing the repeated lies buy into it.

18

THE HATE TRAP

Think of a mouse trap. A thin piece of metal rotates 180 degrees at lightning speed when the bait is eaten. The trap is baited with peanut butter, or other sticky substances mice love.

The mouse takes the bait. In an instant, it's over. The spring does its job.

The Hate Trap is like that, although it traps humans. Hate is the bait. No one would bite on hate, so it must be cleverly disguised as love.

Lies and repeated lies cause confusion. Then more lies get us to take the bait. The solution is offered. As example, abortion makes her life go back to normal. Hate pretends to be love for the panicked mom. It's not. It is hate packaged cleverly as love.

Impostors use the Hate Trap to gain power and authority. They get votes. Then they use their power and authority for our destruction.

(Matthew 18:7) Woe to the world because of the things that cause people to stumble! Such things must come, but woe to the person through whom they come!

Impostors need a mouthpiece apparatus to repeat and protect lies. They have employed national media and enlisted famous people, democratic party officials at the local, state, and national level, knowingly or unknowingly, and get tricked, kind-hearted citizens to join in.

The ones joining in with the impostor spirit repeat the lie on social media and other places.

Impostor elitists plot it all.

Dads in great numbers didn't think their partner would get pregnant. Men, like women, believe the abortion lies. They believe her life goes back to normal after aborting. It's untrue.

Guardians of minors may insist upon an abortion. The girl gets no choice. She is forced.

Truth sets people free. Installing waiting periods and having expectant moms watch truthful videos defeats abortion.

Impostors require elected officials to implement impostor agendas after getting elected. They hide perilous intentions from the public.

Politicians on both sides of the aisle get their legislative bills from impostor-led think tanks. Lobbyists wield power. America does well to end these corrupt relationships.

The federal government is too controlling over state matters. States are too controlling as well. Just look at what was imposed by states during the "pandemic."

Rule of the land needs to be returned to the people. It is unwise to elect politicians who do not support this shift.

Accountability needs to be put in place to track federal and state spending down to the penny. Too much is stolen in today's corrupt systems.

Jesus teaches his followers to serve humanity. The impostor teaches followers to steal, kill, and destroy. It's a stark contrast. Voters can remember this.

Science always confirms God, but impostors twist science to their liking. Today's sophisticated medical equipment defeats the lie that the baby is a blob of tissue.

Girls and women who hear their child's heartbeat begin falling in love with their child; even those pregnant after molestation.

Society struggles with pregnancy after molestation. Truth is hidden. Even after such circumstance, abortion can cause horrific emotional trauma for the mom.

Molested girls may not be emotionally ready or able to keep the child. The willing choose another mom to raise it, so the new mom and baby are blessed by her.

The impostor mom kept lying. She likely had quite a following. I'm sure many in society were stunned after learning who was who. King Solomon's wisdom exposed her, the liar.

I expect it about the same in America. Nothing is new under the sun. King Solomon said so. Liars are being exposed.

Accuse the other side of being racist. Accuse the other side of being hateful. Accuse the other side of being liars. Accuse the other side of being Nazis. It brings many to the side of the impostor because lies repeated often enough become "truth."

Bait cleverly disguised as love trap people and whole classes of people.

Abortion is hatred hidden as love. It is Hate Trap 101. Repeat lies hard and long enough, and the lies pretend to be truth.

At the moment the child is aborted, most moms learn the truth. In their heart they know. What was a lie a moment earlier—no, it isn't a child—is suddenly very clear. Yes, it was. Even those pregnant after molestation.

Weeping girls and women pack the abortion center recovery room, if it can be called that. Rows of chairs are placed about. After the required time, victims are sent away. They exit out a side or back door. Staff do not want the ones waiting for an abortion to see them.

Sorrowful most stay silent. They fear judgment if their abortion is discovered.

Abby Johnson, who experienced her own two abortions, is a former abortion "clinic" director. She now famously speaks all over our country against abortion. She knows what happens at those "clinics." She stands with the unborn.

Her book is titled *Unplanned*, and a movie telling the story bears the same name. She founded a non-profit *And Then There Were None*. The team ministers to abortion workers to help them find new work.

Impostors have erected laws in many states to prevent true root causes of same-sex attraction from being discovered. They hide behind laws they constructed to keep their lies protected. Ministries help individuals to find the true root cause of their gender confusion. It could have been an event or something someone said. These ministries help set people free. People realize what caused their confusion and then begin leading the lives they were meant to live.

Impostors celebrate when someone "comes out." But if someone leaves the lifestyle, they will be verbally attacked if they speak up publicly. It is the Hate Trap in play. Impostors villainize those who speak against their lies.

Impostor-controlled people will refute this. Yet they are the same ones promoting all the bad fruit on the wrong tree. Who should listen to them?

What a voter isn't willing to do before chaos emerges, they may do in the midst of it. People may give up their right to bear arms, give up privacy freedoms, give up freedoms to leave their home, and give up going to church in person. Impostors hate us worshipping the one true God.

Another impostor technique is to use false science and chaos to pass massive spending bills.

Climate change is an example. Impostors use false science to create fear. Then they seek voter approval for huge tax increases.

Climate change fear is manufactured to scare people. Impostors say the world will soon perish. Trillions in tax collection then fund the wrong tree. Much of it is earmarked to wreak havoc all over the globe.

Society seems completely asleep that impostors have a desire and are pushing for a one world government.

Many of the pieces are in place. Impostors know if America falls, their plan is secure.

The national debt will eventually cause bankruptcy if not corrected. Reckless spending does this. Impostors desire our constitution to collapse. Then they form a new government. The right to seize property is likely enacted. The rationale will be to pay off national debt.

Both political parties are contributors. The republican party is infiltrated with many impostors. They work to keep true republicans from working for us, the people, at state and national level.

Purging of corrupt politicians from Washington, DC, started in 2017. Now state governments are exposed too.

Underworld forces apply pressure on officials. People get trapped. Some willingly participate becoming wealthy. Others go along out of fear. Threats, black-mail, and other impostor tools demand alignment to their destructive schemes.

God disagrees with the direction of America. He is raising up a new breed of godly leaders at local, state, and national level. "Legal" overtaxation to steal from Americans is coming to an end. Money is not the only thing impostors steal.

19

TRUTH DEFEATS ABORTION

The abortion battleground is in the legal system. Some bombshell cases have recently come before the US Supreme Court.

Whatever the Supreme Court decides is not enough.

The blood of Abel called out to God.

The blood of Uriah the Hittite did too.

And so does the blood of the unborn.

The impostor will retrench at the State level and also on the internet. Impostors will cling to abortion up to so many weeks.

The abortion snake desires to crawl underground. Black market clinics may emerge. Certainly, mail order abortion pills will attempt to take over.

The FDA is moving forward with permissions to legally distribute abortion pills. Whose side is government on? Life?

School boards are the key to defeating abortion. Truthful, well done, age-appropriate videos can portray the precise information kids need.

School district by school district, the scourge lifts. Future Americans will wonder how people once thought abortion was considered a loving solution to pregnancy.

Moms who experienced physical and emotional trauma have a role. Dads too. Abortion testimonials belong in the video.

Pictures of crying girls and women in the "clinic" recovery rooms belong.

True science about how quickly the embryo forms tiny legs, arms, and heartbeat is necessary.

The awful truth about verifying an abortion should make every American sick. That "blob" of cells must be pieced back together at the abortion clinic to ensure a leg or arm or other body part isn't left in the womb.

Get busy, America. Make videos for our children to watch. They need the full truth.

Pro bono legal services must come alongside school districts. The local church must rise up too. Where is their righteous voice?

In addition, politicians at state and local level have a role. Waiting periods need to be instituted. Videos must be created and watched.

Legislative bodies not willing to enact waiting periods and require expectant moms watch a truthful video are uninterested in defeating abortion.

The truth sets us free. Kids need to hear truth. So does anyone contemplating an abortion.

Girls and women must be sent to pregnancy resource centers during waiting periods. Grandmas, open up your spare bedroom for panicked moms. Many abortion decisions occur due to funding shortages. Go to pregnancy resource centers and put your name on a volunteer list.

New Christian nonprofits are needed to assist finding homes for American babies. Private adaption agencies are motivated by money. Babies are not to be commodities for sale. This needs rapid change.

American history books must document impostor-led atrocities. All the ones mentioned in this book and more, belong in US and outside US history textbooks for classrooms.

The Word is a name of Jesus. The World is a name for the impostor. The "l" represents Lucifer, or in other words, the devil.

Do not be a friend of the World.

(James 4:4)… Therefore, anyone who chooses to be a friend of the world becomes an enemy of God.

God loves sinners. With his whole heart, he wants them to love him back.

Kids need to know how the impostor spirit works to steal free will. Impostors always impose their will on ignorant people. In their elitist impostor view, all humans are ignorant except them.

Hate Trap techniques explain how most of it was done. The full descriptive version is explained in depth in the original version of *Rescue Us Wisdom: Giants Do Fall.*

Children need to know how evil speaks its lies to gain control. Evil uses fear. Look at the freedoms given up during the "pandemic." Churches were closed. Schools were closed. Hair salons were closed. But abortion clinics remained open.

School boards have the power to bring scripture back into the school. Parents and schools can shine wisdom's light.

Kids need to know the story of King Solomon's court. The battle is good versus evil. There is a hidden battle for our children's souls, and ours.

The three R's are important, yes. But what about eternal life and death? The original public school system taught kids to read, so they could read the bible. It was one of the few books a family had in their home.

The wisdom of Solomon needs to be taught in schools.

We are given free will by God. We choose where we will live for eternity. We accept Jesus into our heart, or not. This is the most important decision we make in our life.

We, the people, control what our kids are taught, not the government. If parents want to opt their children out from certain school curriculum, okay. The mainstream should not be controlled by the few.

Law enforcement, if allowed to do their job, squashes black market and internet assisted abortions. Much of it today goes unchecked.

20

THE HEALER

Some physical ailments come from confrontation. After forgiveness the physical symptoms cease.

Some doctors and pastors eighty to a hundred years ago understood this. They searched for a root cause event at the time the symptom began. The prescription was nothing more than a note saying to repeat this or that every day until healing is achieved. Commonly, the physical problem had its root in a quarrelsome situation between people.

The prescription, as example, was to repeat a daily prayer of forgiveness for so and so. After a while the symptoms end. They are cured. Forgiveness healed the person's ailment.

Forgiveness therapy changed hearts too. People befriended the person they previously couldn't tolerate.

When children back then developed cold-like symptoms, some doctors understood its root. Young kids can experience separation anxiety from parents.

Doctors and clergy need to be taught forgiveness therapy.

It seems this understanding has disappeared. Was that on purpose by impostor influence in society to sell more medicine?

The word pharmacy traces to the word *pharmakeus*—which is a drug, poison, charm, spell, or enchantment. Does this sound godly? Impostors use words from their world.

Doctors and clergy can gain new understanding of Jesus the healer. He heals through forgiveness.

Jesus also heals through grace. The words of Isaiah Chapter 53:4–5 (NKJV) say so:

> *Surely He has borne our griefs. And carried our sorrows; Yet we esteemed Him stricken, smitten by God, and afflicted. But He was wounded for our transgressions, He was bruised for our iniquities; The chastisement for our peace was upon Him, And by His stripes we are healed.*

He has borne our griefs is one of the many promises.

The pharmaceutical industry is focused on making money. Many root causes can be treated without medicine. Lots of medicines cause harmful side effects.

Jesus's healing is free. There are no side effects. It is pure and holy. Praise to you, O Lord.

Buried anger harms relationships in various ways.

One way is it leaks out in sarcasm. Messages contain barbs. It's like the recipient gets jabbed with a sharp pin or needle.

Another problem is anger can get internalized. It is pushed down deep. It can cause insecurity and other issues.

A third type of buried anger causes severe outbursts. Pent up anger, pushed down, comes all out at once.

Something triggered it.

God is willing to remove all of our lifetime hurts. He is willing to replace them with joy and peace. Our past can block what He wants to do to give us His best.

Hidden hurts do not need to inflict pain on us anymore. As mentioned earlier, Praying Medic was given a process from the Lord. It is scripture-based. The memory of the hurtful event remains but there is no longer any emotional trauma attached to it.

The Lord's prayer is important. One line says give us this day, our daily bread. Bread has a double meaning. It is food, yes. It is also a reference to Jesus, the bread of life, who is the true manna from Heaven.

There is power in the Lord's Prayer.

> *(Matthew 6:9–13 NKJV) In this manner, therefore, pray: Our Father in heaven, Hallowed be Your name. Your kingdom come. Your will be done, on earth as it is in heaven. Give us this day our daily bread. And forgive us our debts, as we*

forgive our debtors. And do not lead us into temptation but deliver us from the evil one. For Yours is the kingdom and the power and the glory forever. Amen.

Unforgiveness can become poison in one's soul. Jesus said to be forgiven, we must forgive others. Take forgiveness seriously.

It's a daily prayer. We ask for *daily* bread. We're asking for food and Jesus. Later in the prayer it says forgive us, as we forgive others. That is meant to be said daily too.

Revelator Kat Kerr says the anointing talked about in 1 John 2:27 has supernatural power. She says all believers have it. Learn from her about this revelation.

God helps us to let go and let God, to enjoy life in the full. We say out loud, "I choose from my will to forgive others [name them], and I choose from my will to forgive myself."

21

BLESSINGS

A current prophet of God says we should bless God, bless ourselves, then bless a spouse if we have one.

I don't know what it means to bless God. I started doing it anyway. I bless each of the Trinity individually.

Bless Father, bless Son, and bless Holy Spirit.

Why stop there? Bless children, their spouses if they have them, and their children.

Bless friends and extended family.

Sing God bless America. Do it in the shower, or in the car traveling to work.

Bless the seekers. These are ones looking for God, but looking in the wrong places. Among them are new agers who find the counterfeit spirit instead of the Holy Spirit.

The ones earning money from dark sources live lost. Like drug dealers. Or human traffickers. Or pimps. God loves them all. He is the real mom. Jesus is the friend of sinners. When his creation is living with the false mom because she stole them, he deeply misses them.

Bless the seekers and the lost. Pray for them.

(James 1:17) Every good and perfect gift is from above, coming down from the Father of the heavenly lights, who does not change like shifting shadows.

Ask the Lord to deposit a seed of his light into their soul. If it lodges there, the darkness cannot overcome it. There is a Christian song that says it only takes a spark to get a fire going.

Some Christians dabble in new age stuff, like yoga, acupuncture, mediums, Ouija boards, tarot cards, and other practices.

Choose from your will to loosen from your soul all harm done by these things. Then choose from your will to replace them with the spirit of peace and joy.

Exercise is important. Chanting or meditating on a "higher" spirit while doing it is not healthy. Many are unknowingly meditating on the masquerader of light—Lucifer or Satan. Be careful.

(2 Corinthians 11:14) And no wonder, for Satan himself masquerades as an angel of light.

It is most difficult to pray for enemies.

(Matthew 5:43–48) You have heard that it was said, "Love your neighbor and hate your enemy." But I tell you, love your enemies and pray for those who persecute you, that you may be children of your Father in heaven. He causes his sun to rise on the evil and the good, and sends rain on the righteous and the unrighteous. If you love those who love you, what reward will you get? Are not even the tax collectors doing that? And if you greet only your own people, what are you doing more than others? Do not even pagans do that? Be perfect, therefore, as your heavenly Father is perfect.

Humans are unable to be perfect. We strive to understand God's heart and be like him the best we can. Jesus was the role model.

Saul thought he was doing God's work. He was beating and murdering early followers of Jesus two thousand years ago. There are people like Saul living in the world even today. They believe hating Christians is their godly duty. This happens all over the earth, especially Africa, the Middle East, and Far East. Pray that plotters of terror have a supernatural encounter with Jesus. Dreams and visions fall into this category.

Global elitists plot America's destruction with their NWO network. They pay people to accomplish deeds in all kinds of US organizations. Many participate unknowingly. Others aptly comply.

Saul became Paul. It can happen in our times. The one's persecuting many can turn sides. Then they fight with us not against us. Praise God for his mercy. He pursues all.

> *(Ezekiel 33:11) Say to them, "As surely as I live, declares the Sovereign Lord, I take no pleasure in the death of the wicked, but rather that they turn from their ways and live. Turn! Turn from your evil ways! Why will you die, people of Israel?"*

This was written long ago. Back then it applied to the Hebrews. Now it applies to all peoples. Die could mean physical death. It certainly means eternal death.

Impostors convince others to do their dirty work. They stay insulated from their crimes. They think they remain hidden. It's not true.

> *(Hebrews 4:13) Nothing in all creation is hidden from God's sight…*

Time is certainly running out for NWO plotters to repent. Many have chosen hearts of stone and serve the anti-Christ spirit willingly. The Lord has heard our prayers for these enemies of mankind. The move of God to sweep them away is soon at hand.

Impostors have infiltrated the government, media, corporations, entertainment, education, and even the American church at high levels. All things hidden are coming into view. God is bringing His justice.

Anyone on the wrong side of abortion needs to make that correction. Some unknowingly support impostor causes. Others think they can continue to knowingly do those things and get away with it.

When abortion falls, we thank the Lord. We celebrate, celebrate, celebrate. We praise God for rescuing us from this impostor scourge. Jesus, by his wisdom, is the victor.

We cannot be rescued from Hell unless we receive Jesus into our heart. Jesus was the source of King Solomon's wisdom. Rescue us, Jesus, from eternal death, and rescue our nation!

(1 Corinthians 1:24)… Christ the power of God and the wisdom of God.

After World War II, Nazi criminals were helped by the church and by the courts to escape. Let's not make the same mistake. This time should be different. US and global NWO criminals must be brought to justice—and all of their accomplices, from top to bottom.

Bless the tormented Christian brothers and sisters who are beaten and battered by haters in distant lands. They endure extreme trials for the Lord. Find ministries to support them. Pray for them.

Bless the Lord and others with first fruit funds. Set it aside when payday arrives. Perhaps deposit it into a separate checkbook.

Tithing is essential (10 percent of income), but God loves a gracious giver. Recall the widow's two small coins to the church treasury. It was the smallest amount given by anyone but most cherished by Jesus.

She gave all she had. With no money left, she must trust God for food to eat. Few of us have great faith like her. Congregations come beside the tithers with small incomes.

Impostors amassed fortunes by stealing, killing, and destroying. Still, they thirsted for more. God's wealthy will cheerfully give away vast amounts to lift others up.

When excess taxation ends, and even before, it is appropriate for godly owned and operated businesses to give 10 percent back to the Lord. Do good with set-aside funds. Spread God's word or do godly works. Urban centers and lives need rebuilding. Keep this in mind.

Have cash on hand to bless strangers in search of money. Giving to the needy is like blessing the Lord himself. Tell recipients God loves them, because he does.

(Proverbs 19:17) Whoever is kind to the poor lends to the Lord, and he will reward them for what they have done.

22

GIVE GOD THE GLORY

People can be taught to heal, prophesy, give words of wisdom, etc., while others receive anointings for this type of ministry. In the days ahead, more healings will happen exponentially. Those who use those abilities must remember to give God the glory. It is all about him, not about us. No one should think, *Look at the ones being healed through me. I must be going to Heaven.* The following piece of scripture is one of the most difficult Bible passages to read.

> *(Matthew 7:21–23) Not everyone who says to me, "Lord, Lord," will enter the kingdom of heaven, but only the one who does the will of my Father who is in heaven. Many will say to me on that day, "Lord, Lord, did we not prophesy in your name and in your name drive out demons and in your name perform many miracles?" Then I will tell them plainly,*

"I never knew you. Away from me, you evildoers!"

We get to Heaven if we have Jesus alive in our hearts. It is God's grace (free gift) that saves us. Our works do not earn our salvation. Jesus died on the cross to save us. Our work is simply to testify to the Father, Son, and the Holy Spirit. We remain humble and give God the glory.

To receive the free gift of grace, we say a prayer like the following one.

Jesus, I am sorry for my past. Please forgive me. Come into my heart and be my Savior. Teach me your ways. Make me a new creation in you. Amen

After that, we keep Jesus alive in our heart.

The most important commandment according to Jesus is to love God with all of our heart, soul, mind, and strength. The second is similar. We love our neighbor as ourselves.

We strive to make this our lifestyle. Just doing kind acts for someone else is cheered greatly in Heaven. Be kind. Be loving to others, even to those who aren't very likeable. Heaven applauds us when we show kindness.

(Philippians 4:4-5) Rejoice in the Lord always. I will say it again: Rejoice! Let your gentleness be evident to all.

One kindness is to tell friends and family the Lord wants us to have him take hurts from our wounded souls. Our soul is where our memories and emotions reside.

It is like we have a bucket of negative emotions there, containing such things as anger, shame, fear, anxiety, sorrow, grief, and despair. Some of this gets passed on from a previous generation. Some are new from our own experiences.

We carry it around with us. It weighs us down. Think about luggage or a big trunk. The Lord desires to remove it all. He will "take out the trash." Our junk trunk can be emptied.

Heaven is full of joy, peace, and love. We can ask for these emotions to flood our souls. Jesus is willing. It is the soul cleansing process described by Praying Medic and Kat Kerr throughout this book.

23

DESTINY

There are common destinies. Then some unique to us.

Our common destinies are to find Jesus and keep Him alive in our hearts. He loves a joyous giver. He loves when we love the ones needing help. Make being kind a habit.

I believe there are five common destinies. It's a short, simple list:

1. Find Jesus.
2. Repent of sin and accept Him into our heart.
3. Keep Him alive there. Sing praises. Read scripture. Pray. Continual repentance. When we love Jesus, we are loving God.
4. Love your neighbor as yourself. Be kind. When we choose from our will to love our neighbors, including forgiving them, we are loving Jesus.
5. Plant seeds of love and grace so others can find Jesus.

Judgment is the opposite of number five. A club over the head pushes people away from Jesus, not to Him. Be genuine, not pushy. We draw others to him by kindness.

> *(2 Timothy 2:24–26) And the Lord's servant must not be quarrelsome but must be kind to everyone, able to teach, not resentful. Opponents must be gently instructed, in the hope that God will grant them repentance leading them to a knowledge of the truth, and that they will come to their senses and escape from the trap of the devil, who has taken them captive to do his will.*

Doing number three on the list is so important. Be joyful unto the Lord. He loves it!

Our unique destiny is to fulfill our purpose on earth. We have family destinies and occupational destinies. We all have our individual roles.

Continually getting to know God better helps us to find our unique destinies. God desires our affection. He hopes for a two-way, personal relationship.

Items one to three in the list are the most important. We accept Jesus and keep Him alive in our heart. Our eternity depends upon it. Points four and five become outgrowths of doing lines one through three.

24

ONCE SAVED, ALWAYS SAVED?

What is true is God will not forsake us. That means he'll never leave us. Jesus will stay in our heart as long as we want him to.

People get busy. They forget about Him. Difficulty comes. People reject Jesus because of pressure. Bad things happen and people lose faith.

We must protect our mind and heart.

God will never leave us, but people leave him. The evil one snatches Jesus from us. It is the parable of the sower. Read of it in Matthew 13.

On the night of the last supper, Jesus warned his closest followers in John 15:1–6. He is the true vine. Some branches wither. Then the dead branches are burned. Unfortunately, doesn't this mean the ones that give up on Jesus spend eternity in the lake of fire?

(John 15:6) If you do not remain in me,
you are like a branch that is thrown away

*and withers; such branches are picked up,
thrown into the fire and burned.*

If Jesus warned his disciples of this, it is a warning to all.

Then he warned them again.

(John 16:1) All this I have told you so that you will not fall away.

In addition to Jesus's warnings, Apostle Paul talked about people's faith becoming shipwrecked. This is imagery of disaster.

Once saved, always saved is only true if we keep Jesus alive in our hearts. Stay attached to Jesus.

If a person was hurt by people in the church, then attend online. Read your bible. Pray. But get reconnected. Sing to the Lord. Renew your vows.

Jesus, forgive my sins. Enter my heart and make me a new creation in you. Amen.

Going to church doesn't save someone. Church isn't a box to check off to show living a "good" lifestyle.

(Luke 13:25–28) Once the owner of the house gets up and closes the door, you will stand outside knocking and pleading, "Sir, open the door for us." But he will answer, "I don't know you or where you come from."

Then you will say, "We ate and drank with you, and you taught in our streets." But he will reply, "I don't know you or where you come from. Away from me, all you evildoers!" There will be weeping there, and gnashing of teeth, when you see Abraham, Isaac and Jacob and all the prophets in the kingdom of God, but you yourselves thrown out.

Here are probable keys to understand the story.

House = Heaven.
Owner of the House = God.
Door = Heaven's gate = Jesus.
Street = Church.
Eat and drink = Communion.

This parable says to me people go to church and take communion, but they do not have Jesus in their heart. The door of Heaven will be closed to them.

What is the fear of the Lord? Many say it is the fear of eternal separation from God. We have a fear of not going to Heaven. Others say it is fear of doing something that displeases the Lord. Perhaps it is both.

Does the reader fear separation from God? There is no need to fear if your name is written in the book of life. Is the reader saved? Is Jesus in your heart?

God gives us free will. It is a choice we get to make. Accept wisdom or reject it. Accept Jesus into one's heart and keep him alive there or not. It is life's most important choices.

Teachers of the Word do well if they remind parishioners of the fear of the Lord.

> *(Proverbs 1:7) The fear of the Lord is the beginning of knowledge, but fools despise wisdom and instruction.*

It's not a fire and brimstone message. It simply means Hell exists. People choose where they spend eternity.

A reminder to parishioners is a simple message. There are two camps. Have Jesus in our hearts or not. It is that basic.

Let's review the list again of our common destinies.

I believe there are five common destinies. It's a short, simple list:

1. Find Jesus.
2. Repent of sin and accept Him into our heart.
3. Keep Him alive there. Sing praises. Read scripture. Pray. Continual repentance. When we love Jesus, we are loving God.
4. Love your neighbor as yourself. Be kind. When we choose from our will to love our neighbors, including forgiving them, we are loving Jesus.

5. Plant seeds of love and grace, so others can find Jesus.

Prayer is simply having a conversation with God. He knows our thoughts as they form. Speak them to him anyway, either out loud or silently.

He loves when we talk to him about every aspect of our life. Conversation with God pleases him.

People have unique destinies. If it includes gifts of wisdom, prophecy, prayer language, healing, or other gifts, keep the common destinies in the forefront.

Keeping Jesus alive in our heart is necessary. Grace saves. Doing good works does not. We do good works to show love like Jesus. Our motivation is not because we have to. We do it because we want to. We love because He first loved us.

> *(1 John 4:19) We love because he first loved us.*

> *(Ephesians 2:8-9) For it is by grace you have been saved, through faith—and this is not from yourselves, it is the gift of God— not by works, so that no one can boast.*

25

THE CHURCH BODY

The Lord loves us gathering at his house to praise him and his Son. He desires genuine love and affection from us.

We go to church to sing praises. We go to hear the Word taught. We go to partake in the Lord's supper (communion). We fellowship with other believers. We help bear each other's burdens.

Healings and miracles are breaking out all over America. Find out about them. Congregations should be talking about God's power moving in present times.

Altar calls can be offered each service or meeting. Salvation is the greatest gift of the Lord.

> *(John 5:24) Very truly I tell you, whoever hears my word and believes him who sent me has eternal life and will not be judged but has crossed over from death to life.*

Many have been hurt by church judgment or something else encountered there. They abstain from attending, unfortunately, risking eternal harm. The very place to connect them to the Lord repelled them. It's very sad indeed.

Get reconnected. Watch services online or on television. Read scripture. Meditate on scripture. That means read the bible and ponder what it means. Our subconscious works on it in the background.

Pray. Love God and love your neighbor as yourself. Be kind. Be all the positive things you didn't experience in the church. Be a light to others.

Pastors do well to remove legalism and liberalism from teachings.

Legalism, the traditions of men, is present in some congregations. Do this, don't do that. If you do this or don't do that, a person won't go to Heaven or will go to Hell.

No set of rules can save us. Not even trying our best to follow the ten commandments can do it.

We can't avoid Hell by following rules either.

We are unable to save ourselves by anything we do. People think, I do not do this or that. I am basically a good person. I will go to Heaven.

It's not true.

There is only one way to go to Heaven and thereby avoid Hell.

(John 11:25) Jesus said to her, "I am the resurrection and the life. The one who believes in me will live, even though they die;"

Liberalism is taking church doctrine and bending it to accept modern culture, like abortion. We minister to all people. We love all. God does. But we stay clear of embracing false teachings.

Words spoken by believers inside or outside the church building can be harshly judgmental. God loves everyone. Loving others like he loves us, with gentleness and kindness, draws hurting people to him.

Jesus knows hearts. He weeps with compassion for the brokenhearted. He is gentle toward the lost, tricked and all. His grace forgives our mistakes and urges us to forgive others. Then He remembers them no more. Love and truth without judgment is our top priority.

(Ephesians 4:29 & 32) Do not let any unwholesome talk come out of your mouths, but only what is helpful for building others up according to their needs, that it may benefit those who listen. Be kind and compassionate to one another, forgiving each other, just as in Christ God forgave you.

Some church leaders say bible stories are myth. Some say Hell doesn't exist, and if it does, few people go there.

Some congregations accept all kinds of earthly rules about punishing divorcees, remarrying, paying money for redemption, etc.

Legalism and liberalism don't belong in the church.

There are cults existing that pretend to be godly. Adultery and other deceptive acts can be demanded by leadership. Jesus never condones this behavior.

Some TV ministries promise tremendous godly favor by giving seed money to their ministries. Be careful. Two thousand years ago, it was going on too. Apostle Paul contrasts himself to others.

> *(2 Corinthians 2:17) Unlike so many, we do not peddle the word of God for profit. On the contrary, in Christ we speak before God with sincerity, as those sent from God.*

Some branches struggle with the Trinity. There is the Father, Son, and Holy Spirit. It is truth. Many, many scripture verses talk about each of them.

In our time the Lord has released easy to understand descriptors of the Trinity through a seven-year-old child of God.

Perhaps most fifth graders should be able to grasp these Trinity concepts. Thank you, Lord. We have been confused.

These are from Josiah Cullen:

He is Papa (Father).
He is Healer (Son).
He is Helper (Holy Spirit).
Here's how the world began:
The Father thought it.
The Son loved it.
The Holy Spirit carried out the plan.

Another concept:
The Father is the manager.
The Son is the lover of operations.
The Holy Spirit is the worker.
It's the three-in-one getting things done.
So man must voice (the questions):
Father, what do you think?
Son, what do you love?
Holy Spirit, what should we do about it?
That's our mission.

I hope readers are richly blessed by what the Lord has provided through Josiah. We can apply the last portion to the American Church.

Father, what do you think?
Son, what do you love?

Holy Spirit, what should we do about it?

Much in this chapter is taking aim at the very question.

Some mediate through a person who is not deity.

> *(1 Timothy 2:5) For there is one God and one mediator between God and mankind, the man Christ Jesus.*

Some "church" leaders expect sexual favors to be performed by members. Some promote adultery to obtain personal gratification. Those teaching or practicing them do not have the Spirit of God guiding them.

Some teach we can become gods ourselves.

Some claiming to represent God hold onto membership through threats of harm. This type of behavior is not from God.

Some teach it is okay to sin as much as an individual wants to because by grace it is excused. This is not true.

> *(Romans 6:1–2) What shall we say, then? Shall we go on sinning so that grace may increase? By no means!...*

The different terms and practices of the righteous church can be confusing.

Infant baptism is practiced by some and not others. Baptism brings the gift of the Holy Spirit. Why not give the gift at an early age?

Some use the term born-again. Others don't. It's confusing. Jesus never said, your faith has reborn you. He said your faith saves you. This isn't meant to be criticism. Christian jargon of some confuse other Christians.

Aren't we reborn the day we leave earth for Heaven?

Infants baptized go through confirmation classes as teenagers for a year or two. Pastoral teachings can be wonderful. Kids prosper with understanding. But if Jesus is not in their heart, knowledge is meaningless.

In terms of confirming faith, why not use altar calls instead? A child does so when ready unless pressured by adults which shouldn't be. Too many kids go through the motion at the confirmation service. It's like they graduate from church.

Anyone can accept faith by saying a prayer to fill their heart with Jesus. Say—*Jesus forgive me. Come into my heart and be my Savior. I praise you. Amen.*

The church does well if top level doctrine agrees. The early church adopted the Apostles Creed. Many still follow it centuries later.

There is a prevailing view once saved, always saved. Scripture is clear Jesus will never leave us. But scripture is also clear people can walk away from faith.

(Colossians 1:22–23) But now he has reconciled you by Christ's physical body through death to present you holy in his sight, without blemish and free from accusation—if you continue in your faith, established and firm, and do not move from the hope held out in the gospel....

Verse 23 places an "if" squarely upon us. We must continue in our faith.

Communion can be denied to believers of other denominations who visit churches of other denominations. Why?

Christians are Christians. If a person professes Jesus as their Lord and Savior, why are they treated as second class by a brother or sister in Messiah Jesus?

The body of Jesus has many parts. If a denomination is a "foot," then the "hand" is not permitted to be fed in "your" house? Isn't it the Father's house?

(1 Corinthians 12:15) Now if the foot should say, "Because I am not a hand, I do not belong to the body," it would not for that reason stop being part of the body.

Why isn't a child able to be fed at the table? There is power in communion. Jesus said let the children come unto me.

Some offer communion every week. Others once a month. Why the differences? Isn't being fed an act of remembering him? It is connected to his passion. The words of Isaiah 53: 4–5 belong in communion services. His power can be released during communion.

> *(Isaiah 53:4–5 NKJV) Surely He has borne our griefs, And carried our sorrows; Yet we esteemed Him stricken, Smitten by God, and afflicted. But He was wounded for our transgressions, He was bruised for our iniquities; The chastisement for our peace was upon Him, And by His stripes we are healed.*

Jesus's passion carries our sorrows. He bears our grief. He heals us by his stripes. This is in addition to forgiving our sins and saving us for eternity. All of this should be remembered when receiving the Lord's supper (communion).

The words currently used from Matthew are important. So are the words of Isaiah 53 4–5 to remember His power. The words of Isaiah 52:13–15, His Passion, are to be remembered too:

> *See, my servant will act wisely; he will be raised and lifted up and highly exalted. Just as there were many who were appalled at him—his appearance was so disfigured*

beyond that of any human being and his form marred beyond human likeness—so he will sprinkle many nations, and kings will shut their mouths because of him. For what they were not told, they will see, and what they have not heard, they will understand.

The Lord's supper is meant to release his power. All of this can be remembered while taking communion.

Can someone go to Heaven in the spirit and return? Lazarus died. His body was in the tomb. Even after four days, his spirit returned to him. He lived on earth again.

How did the transfiguration occur? God brought the spirit of Moses and Elijah to talk with Jesus.

If God did those things, he can bring someone's spirit into Heaven and return it to earth. He is God. Because someone says they went to Heaven does not make it so. But because someone says they went to Heaven does not make it false. It happens more frequently than people realize.

Revelator Kat Kerr has been in Heaven countless times in the spirit. Pastor Don Piper was in Heaven in the spirit too. So was Pastor Henry Gruver. Each of them wrote books about it.

A young boy visited Heaven as well. His dad, Todd Burpo, with Lynn Vincent documented the event in the book *Heaven is for Real.*

Around the same time an eight-year-old artist painted a masterpiece painting of Jesus. Todd's son Colten said the painting represents exactly what Jesus looks like.

Todd speaks all over the US about his son's experience. He shows audiences a photo of the painting. Hundreds upon hundreds tell Todd after giving his testimony the picture is accurate. They, too, have been in Heaven in the spirit. They agree it is what Jesus looks like.

God wants people to know Heaven is real. He also wants people to know Hell exists. Some clergy deny there is a Hell. Or if there is a Hell, few people go there. Didn't Jesus himself say find the narrow path? He said wide is the path that leads to destruction. Whose side are Hell deniers on? They deny the truths of Jesus.

Clergy of various denominations do well if they collaborate with each other. Adopt best practices. Purge the falsehoods. Then the American Church centers itself in the fullness of grace and truth.

God is pouring out spirit-filled gifts upon the earth. Learn about healing, prophecy, speaking in tongues, getting words of knowledge and wisdom, and other gifts.

Speaking in tongues is becoming mainstream. Recent news suggests half of American churchgoers have received this gift. Does the full American Church know this? Why not? Is it because congregations don't talk to each other?

On the other hand, some think if a person doesn't speak in tongues, a person isn't filled with the Holy Spirit. Some continue incorrect thought even further. They suggest a person without tongues may not be saved. That's a problematic, unbiblical view.

The Lord did not say believe in my Son and demonstrate it by speaking in tongues to have eternal life.

Legalism is sneaky. A person does not need to speak in tongues to go to Heaven.

Shouldn't congregations have elders who heal what medicines don't? Apostle Paul talked about it. It was expected in his day. What happened?

Healings occur in spirit-filled congregations. Don't all congregations desire to operate in the gifts?

Greater works are manifesting on earth. The lame walk. People receive new hearts and other body parts supernaturally. Our God is a gracious God. Of course, the media hides these things. They are on the side of abortion, not God.

Why don't all Christian kids and adults understand the power of a sinner's prayer?

Becoming saved by Jesus does happen by saying one. First, a person confesses they have been apart from God. Then they say they are sorry for their sins. Lastly, they invite Jesus into their heart. They receive him as their Savior.

Jesus told the gospel (good news) to an almost four-year-old. I thank Colten Burpo, his dad Todd, Lynn

Vincent, and Jesus for the wonderful book *Heaven is for Real.*

Colten visited Heaven two months before his fourth birthday. He momentarily died during appendectomy surgery. Then went into Heaven.

While there, Jesus told the lad—I died so people can come see my dad. Then he informed Colten people need to have Jesus in their heart to go to Heaven.

Wow. The gospel preached to Colten by Jesus shows how simple it can be.

After Colten believed, the Lord showed him revelation. No one looks old in Heaven. The unborn are adopted by Jesus's dad. The unborn are excited for their parents to arrive someday.

The good news isn't complicated. At death, those who have Jesus in their heart are reborn to Heaven. It's so basic. Thank you, Jesus, for the gospel and revelation given to Colten. It was so simple, a four-year-old understood it.

The Lord's Prayer and Apostles Creed are powerful declarations of faith. I'm grateful I grew up with them. They embed Jesus deeply in one's heart. Congregations need these.

Learning to be compassionate like Jesus is important for any follower of Him. Training is needed.

As mentioned earlier, Cindy McGill wrote a book titled *Words That Work.* It's a fantastic writing. Equipping the congregation in understanding God's unsaved friends is essential.

People need to shield seekers from scorn and ridicule. Their artistic gifts and expressions require appreciation. Artistic seekers can need something very different than standard Christian tradition and jargon.

The good Samaritan took that beaten, robbed, half dead man to an inn. The inn may represent His house. Or in other words, a Christian congregation.

The world has their hospitals. They are not free. Jesus's healing costs nothing.

Communion to release Jesus's power per Matthew, Isaiah 52 and 53, and laying on hands are tools to use.

We remove barriers at the houses of the Lord. People need Jesus. He is the friend of sinners. We strive to be welcoming like him. New agers are his friends. Many have turned to the counterfeit one. They require gentle redirection.

Learn to welcome all and provide compassion and healing as Jesus would.

People and congregations can receive more of the Holy Spirit to advance God's will on earth. Luke 11:13 says—*How much more will your Father in heaven give the Holy Spirit to those who ask him!*

Members of the church body choose from their will to stand for the Lord. We can take ground for the kingdom to occupy. Literally, ground means ground.

We occupy every level of government and all rungs of society, including media, entertainment, education, and corporations. Then we stand firm. Jesus gave us this authority. God expects us to use it.

26

RULING AND REIGNING

Revelator Kat Kerr is teaching the American Church (and everyone anywhere) how to rule and reign. Each Jesus follower who understands God's will can command Host from Heaven. We wage war on darkness by authority from the Lord.

Believers can become purposely dangerous to impostor spirit. Jesus was fierce toward the enemy. He rattled the infected religious establishment. Some taught false views. Others became super legalist to follow rules or traditions of men.

Jesus defeated death. Then he gave us access to his power and authority to do the same.

Recall the prodigal son story. The obedient son was told by the Father, everything I have is yours. The Father God has power. That means each obedient believer shares His power.

We have power to vote. Power to change our hearts. Power to speak. Power to pray. Power to fast. Power to declare and decree with authority. Power to command

Host into spiritual battle. We can seek supernatural power to heal. We can decree and declare a person be made whole. We can seek words of His knowledge to minister. We have power to move our hands and feet to do his will on earth.

Wisdom reveals truth. Wisdom emboldens truth too. We use wisdom to take ground for the kingdom. We occupy. Rise up American church!

We take care of the orphan. We lift up the broken. The widow is provided for, not from government. The compassionate church cares for its membership and broader community. We share each other's burdens. We love like He first loved us.

Government transitions away from entitlements. Over taxation ends. People work to provide for themselves. They can now afford to live divorced from government oppression. Businesses and congregations perhaps provide child care. Some spouses simply stay at home to raise children.

God-fearing organizations and congregations provide for the needy, not government. America got into this mess by trusting impostor government, not God.

(Proverbs 28:5) Evildoers do not understand what is right, but those who seek the Lord understand it fully.

Some cultures have three generations under one roof. The elderly care for the children while the younger couple works. Impostors have convinced Americans to turn to government for help. Other cultures find ways to adapt without government help.

The Father commanded us to first seek him, and then he will provide what we need.

> *(Matthew 6:31–33) So do not worry, saying, 'What shall we eat?' or 'What shall we drink?' or 'What shall we wear?' For the pagans run after all these things, and your heavenly Father knows that you need them. But seek first his kingdom and his righteousness, and all these things will be given to you as well.*

We sever the bond between false god government and the people. In its place we decentralize government, and government aligns itself to the will of the Father.

Our national government focuses on national security issues. Its focus is to protect the nation and protect infrastructure. Impostors infiltrated us and consolidated power at state and national levels. They've worked to enslave us.

Kat Kerr teaches how to speak mighty decrees. Out loud, we release powerful declarations. Here is an example from her. We say something like this over a troubled individual. Fill in the three blanks with their name.

Father, I declare that _____ will know Jesus Christ. I declare they will know Him and become a Christian, that they will not lose their destiny which _____ was chosen for in Jesus's name, and I come against all the power of Hell that's kept _____ in bondage. I release the anointing into that situation so the (evil) yoke is broken off of them. Amen and amen.

Before leaving home in the morning we can speak a degree. Here is an example.

I will not tolerate darkness around me, against me, or against my family, in Jesus's name. Amen.

Over our friends and loved ones we can speak a declaration such as this one.

I declare that all of my family, my friends, and those that I love will become mighty children of God. They will be free in Jesus's name. They will not lose their destiny. They will become the living testimony of the saving power of Jesus Christ. Amen.

These are just a few examples. Congregations are learning how to teach decrees to parishioners. This must expand.

Ruling and reigning is our God-given right. We take authority. Resist the devil, and he will flee from us.

Kat says believers receive an anointing. She references 1 John 2:27. Learn from her what this means.

Ruling and reigning includes standing for those apart from the Lord. We continue to pray, decree, and declare over them to the end. Our God is a compassionate God. He does the impossible. Kat Kerr says our compassionate God may even intervene at the point of someone's death on our behalf because of prayers.

27

SUMMARY

There was a court case long ago. The real mom and impostor mom argued over a child.

That child in our "modern" times is the innocent one in the womb. The thief desires to steal it from the mom. The impostor mom stands in American courts just like she did in King Solomon's court three thousand years ago. She desires the child cut in two.

That child is also you and me. We can live with the liar devil and die with him. We descend to his hideous torture chamber called Hell.

Lies create confusion. When wisdom clears up confusion, then the choice is clear. We accept or reject wisdom, which means accept Jesus or reject him.

Jesus came to earth. He died for our sins. Accepting him into our hearts is the most important decision of our life. The next most important decision is to keep him alive there.

Jesus said we recognize good and evil by the fruit on the tree. Abortion is bad fruit. So is all the fruit on that tree. Science is always on God's side, but impostors twist science to fool people. Then fooled people trust false science.

Impostors say trust the science. These same ones promote abortion. And climate change. They protect the porn industry. Impostors allow teaching about false gods in school, but won't teach about the true God. They push evolution theory as truth. Theory means it isn't proven. Schools at all levels are pushing impostor falsehoods on our kids.

Impostors switch up lies when their lies get exposed. They said a fetus is a blob of tissue. Science proves them wrong. A heartbeat is already present in three weeks. Impostors now say it is her body, so she can choose.

Scripture is clear. We receive Jesus into our heart for salvation. Then our bodies are no longer our own. Jesus paid for us on the cross.

Impostor science is twisted to shape narratives. It is shifting sand.

Impostors promote free crack pipes for the poor. They push marijuana. They push safe drug zones to legally take drugs. They push experimental vaccines. They say trust the science while insisting wimpy paper masks stop the spread.

Jesus was very clear. The good tree has only good fruit. The bad, only bad.

Republican politicians, in name only, have infiltrated at all levels of government. It will be interesting to watch them. Whoever of them block waiting periods and truthful videos prior to an abortion stymie truth.

Roll call votes bring exposure. Or if no roll call is permitted, that reveals corruption too. The leadership is not acting for us, the people.

Learn from prohibition. Outlawing liquor only caused cheap imitations. Many went blind or died from bathtub booze. Corruption flourished. It was a sorry time in America.

Outlawing abortion will push it likewise underground. Online abortion kits will harm more moms than present abortion methods. Backroom black-market "butcher shops" will perform haphazard baby extraction. Moms will be badly maimed.

Kids need truth. So do moms considering an abortion. What defeats abortion it is giving expectant moms truth, and then providing a volunteer system to assist moms financially.

(John 8:32) "Then you will know the truth, and the truth will set you free."

Government is supposed to be honest.

Children in school watching truthful videos will wonder how previous Americans could ever believe abortion was compassionate.

The original *Rescue Us Wisdom* book has much more scripture and detail about how impostors operate.

Where is the American Church's righteous voice? Why is the church so confused? Embrace wisdom, American Church. Be the voice you are called to be.

Josiah Cullen says faith is picture it done.

Picture it done: abortion falls. Let the American Civil War Against Humanity end. Praise Jesus for the victory! Glory be to God!

Picture it done: post-abortive moms and dads have their broken hearts restored.

Picture it done: the porn industry crumbles to dust.

Picture it done: racial injustice ends.

Picture it done: financial independence comes to all. Let the righteous church body of the Lord be our help and not the false god government.

Reclaim your cherished peoples, Lord. Sever the grip of the oppressors. Be a lamp unto the feet of the oppressed. Lead them to your victory in Messiah Jesus.

Lord Jesus, stand and calm the storm in our cities. Impostors have orchestrated urban destruction. Bring your peace and justice, Lord.

Picture it done: our nation repents and becomes a Godly nation worshipping the Almighty God. Let us give Him honor, glory, praise, and adoration for his loving kindness and promises of life in the full.

Be bound in your own chains, Satan.

America has tried it her way. Return to the Lord, the giver of light, truth, and the way. Unify America. Thank you, Jesus.

Join hands urban, suburban, and rural Americans. Unite in the Lord our God. Vote in primary elections. Defeat the impostors in government. Too many established infiltrators remain too, on the other side. Vote in state and national elections. Decentralize government.

In all ways honor the Sabbath, not going our own way. Employers, end policies forcing workers to work on Son Day or else be fired. Construct policies to honor the Lord.

If an essential service, such as clergy, health services, fire, police, and similar functions, provide a suitable different day for them to pay homage to the Lord.

Many businesses and sports franchises should simply close for the day. They are not essential businesses. Their workers deserve the day off to spend with the Lord and family.

Sport teams survived a whole year without admission sales. Are expensive gate prices and concessions to restrict the poor from attending? They have explaining to do. Greed is greed. Token "poor" sections as a solution would be pitiful.

Society should honor the Lord on his Sabbath Day. Is God our God? How are individuals showing it?

Picture it done: the educational system kindergarten through college/university, all levels, turn away from indoctrinating falsehoods into children.

Picture it done: the motion picture industry turns from its violent representation of modern life. Let their night turn to dawn. Thank you, Lord Jesus.

Picture it done: America in all ways keeps the Sabbath holy.

Picture it done: Media at local and national level turn from extolling darkness to celebrating life! News encourages and builds up society. Stories are full of grace and truth. Darkness is exposed. Thank-you Lord! Hallelujah!

Picture it done: America's corporations honor the Lord. Many oppress their work forces. Some pretend to be upright yet are not. They hide harmful things in their products. They also keep hidden things that can benefit mankind. God knows their secrets. Do corporate leaders and their board of directors fear the Lord?

28

OUR REBORN NATION

Our nation is being reborn. The covert impostor spirit is exposed. God's hand is moving. Injustice is being replaced with justice.

Our flag is full of five-point stars. The stripes have meaning. Are they connected to impostor control? The five-point star is the worship symbol of Satan.

It's appropriate for a new flag to mark our nation's rebirth. What does God think? What does Jesus love? Holy Spirit, what should we do about it?

Our flag clearly should point to God. According to Revelator Kat Kerr, the six-point star symbol on the Israeli flag is all over Heaven. Heaven's version is found on her website.

One triangle represents the Father, Son, and Holy Spirit. The other triangle denotes the body, soul, and spirit of man. The intertwined triangles represent unity of God with people. Why not place it on our flag?

Being a reborn nation begs the question about selecting a new national anthem. Many believe it should be America the Beautiful.

There are war memorials all over America for past conflicts. The American Civil War Against Humanity deserves memorials too. Each US state should find a suitable place on public grounds to honor the unborn victims of abortion.

The numbers are shocking. Over sixty-three million Americans have lost their life in the war against the unborn.

Hardest hit was Hispanic and African Americans. Nearly one-third of minority children perished. All nationalities suffered horrific losses. European descendants in this country account for more than half of the aborted American babies.

Jesus is the one who rescues us. He rescues us individually and our nation. Wisdom defeats abortion. It also defeats all the bad fruit on the wrong tree. The Son glorifies the Father, and the Father glorifies the Son.

A picture of Jesus belongs in our White House for all invited public to see.

We know what he looks like. A copy of artist Akiane Kramarik's *Prince of Peace* masterpiece belongs in our nation's capital and all state capital buildings.

They should be ordered from her gallery, so she receives the funds. Her masterpiece was stolen from her, and others have profited by reproducing its image.

This should not be.

She was finally reunited with it. It is now in safe-keeping somewhere, owned by a private family.

She painted it at age eight. Incredible. Learn her story.

Statues of Jesus belong in every town and city. So do ten commandment monuments. Separation of church and government is an impostor spirit lie. The ten commandments provide a moral code. Honoring them is important. Jesus by his grace and truth saves us. His statue next to the ten commandments reminds us of that.

I believe we each have five common destinies. It's a short, simple list:

1. Find Jesus.
2. Repent of sin and accept Him into our heart.
3. Keep Him alive there. Sing praises. Read scripture. Pray. Continual repentance. When we love Jesus, we are loving God.
4. Love your neighbor as yourself. Be kind. When we choose from our will to love our neighbors, including forgiving them, we are loving Jesus.
5. Plant seeds of love and grace, so others can find Jesus.

People have unique destinies too. We have a contribution to make to society. When we need help, we thank God when we receive it. Society provides it, not government. After we get back on our feet, we work in whatever capacity we are able.

Leaders at all levels and occupations in America lead by godly obedience. Remember always:

> The Father is the manager.
> The Son is the lover of operations.
> The Holy Spirit is the worker.
> It's the three-in-one getting things done.

So, man must voice (the questions):

> Father, what do you think?
> Son, what do you love?
> Holy Spirit, what should we do about it?
> That's our mission.

In all ways as a nation we point to our source of life. In America we honor God the Father, Son, and Holy Spirit. Hallelujah.

> *(Psalm 48:14) For this God is our God for ever and ever; he will be our guide even to the end.*

APOSTLES' CREED

(Q & A as it appears on the Billy Graham Evangelistic Association website)

Q:
What is the Apostles' Creed?
A:

The Apostles' Creed, though not written by the apostles, is the oldest creed of the Christian church and is the basis for others that followed. Its most used form is:

> *I believe in God the Father Almighty, Maker of heaven and earth, And in Jesus Christ his only Son our Lord, Who was conceived by the Holy Ghost, Born of the Virgin Mary, Suffered under Pontius Pilate, Was crucified, dead, and buried. He descended into hell; The third day He rose again from the dead; He ascended into heaven, And sit-teth on the right hand of God the Father Almighty;*

From thence he shall come to judge the quick and the dead. I believe in the Holy Ghost; The Holy catholic Church, the Communion of Saints; The Forgiveness of sins; The Resurrection of the body, And the Life everlasting. Amen.

In its oldest form, the Apostles' Creed goes back to at least 140 AD. Many of the early church leaders summed up their beliefs as they had an opportunity to stand for their faith—see, for example, 1 Timothy 6:12. These statements developed into a more standard form to express one's confession of faith at the time of baptism. It is not Scripture, but it is a simple list of the great doctrines of the faith.

The word "catholic" means "relating to the church universal" and was the word used in the original version of the Creed. It does not mean the Roman Catholic Church, but the church, the body of Christ, as a universal fellowship. The phrase, "He descended into hell," was not part of the creed in its earliest form.

Twaccoont@hofmail.com

Printed in the USA
CPSIA information can be obtained
at www.ICGtesting.com
JSHW082022260923
48886JS00001B/46